Illustrations of Nineteenth Century Sheffield

from Pawson and Brailsford's

'Illustrated Guide to Sheffield'

(1862, 1879, 1889, 1899)

Adrian Middleton

2014

Edition 1 – 2014

Published by Adrian Middleton, 2014
(middlea.jimdo.com)

Paperback edition printed by CreateSpace
(www.createspace.com)

Contents

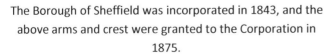

The Borough of Sheffield was incorporated in 1843, and the above arms and crest were granted to the Corporation in 1875.

Sheffield was granted the new arms and crest shown above in 1893, and was elevated by Royal Charter to the status of a City in 1897.

Acknowledgements

This project could not have been undertaken without access to copies of the original 'Illustrated Guides to Sheffield'. Grateful thanks are due to Museums Sheffield (MS), where the present author works as a volunteer, and to Sheffield Local Studies Library. MS staff provided encouragement and enabled access to their collections, specifically to the 1862, 1879 and 1899 editions of the Guide. The Sheffield Local Studies Library has copies of all four editions, including the 1889 edition, and, as well as being ever helpful, allowed access to photograph those illustrations unique to the 1889 volume. The 1889 illustrations on pages 45, 46, 58, 73, 76, 93, 96, 110 and 113 are courtesy of Sheffield Archives and Local Studies. All other images are courtesy of Museums Sheffield.

I would like to thank Natalie Patel and Sue Graves on the Visual Arts team at Museums Sheffield for their help in identifying the artists and engravers listed in the Preface. Thanks are also due to those staff and volunteers who collected the artist information which now resides in the museum's catalogue database – I make no claim that this is my original research.

I would also like to thank the Foljambe family for their help in confirming that the Beauchief Altar-piece (p115) is still in their care, and Maria Sienkiewicz of the Barclays Group Archives for information about the Birmingham, District and Counties Bank (p45).

Finally, I would like to thank those who have contributed to books, web-sites, Wikipedia articles, etc., too numerous to list. Some are shown in the Bibliography, others are still out there waiting to be discovered.

The arms and crest of the Cutlers' Company, more correctly 'The Company of Cutlers in Hallamshire', were granted in 1875. The central bar reflects the arms of the town, and later the City, of Sheffield, the swords relate to the making of edged tools, and to the arms previously shared with the Worshipful Company of Cutlers in London. The motto 'Pour Y Parvenir A Bonne Foi' (To succeed through good faith) in also derived from that of the London cutlers.

Preface

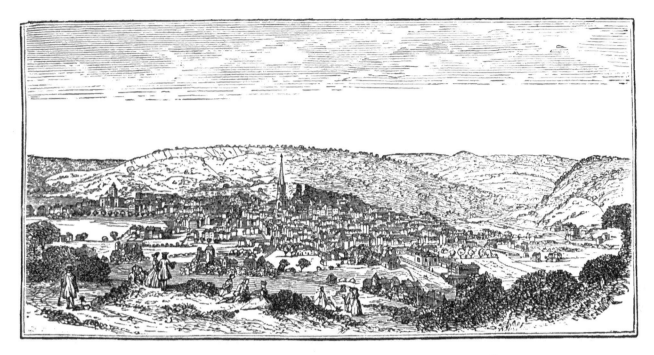

VIEW OF SHEFFIELD FROM PARK HILL IN 1740.

Through the Eighteenth and Nineteenth Centuries, the citizens of Sheffield, or at least those who could read, would have had access to a series of Directories which would outline the history, prominent buildings and character of the town in which they lived and carried out their business. The directories would list the important citizens, the professionals and the trades-people, giving their addresses and a variety of other information of use to their readers.

The Illustrated Guides

The view of Sheffield shown above is taken from what was a new type of book – an Illustrated Guide – in this case, the 'Illustrated Guide to Sheffield and the Surrounding District' published in 1879 by a local publisher – Pawson and Brailsford – and edited by John Taylor. To give it its full title, it was the 'Illustrated Guide to Sheffield and the Surrounding District comprising accounts of the early history and progress of the town, its public and religious bodies, edifices and institutions, descriptions of its manufactures, and of the suburban scenery and places of interest in the surrounding district, &c.'.

The view was based on the 'East Prospect of Sheffield', a copperplate engraving produced by Samuel and Nathaniel Buck, and generally dated 1745. By 1879, the view was totally outdated, being over 130 years old. During that time the town had expanded considerably, and much that had previously been countryside was now covered by housing, steel-works, railways, canals, and by a pall of smoke.

The first edition of the 'Guide' had appeared in 1862 (without the above illustration), and was an early production of the newly formed partnership of 'Pawson and Brailsford', formed three years earlier. Henry Pawson had served his apprenticeship as a printer, and worked on the 'Leeds Intelligencer' (later the 'Yorkshire Post'). He came to Sheffield as a reporter on the 'Sheffield Times', and in 1853 he bought the paper with a partner, Samuel Harrison, but their partnership ended in 1858 with Harrison continuing the newspaper business. Joseph Brailsford, a native of Sheffield, had worked for some years on the 'Sheffield and Rotherham Independent'.

In 1859 Pawson and Brailsford took over the business of Broomhead Greaves Rogers which included the Britannia Printing Office in Castle Street and a shop and works 'at the Church Gate' (seen on p14). The Britannia Works were later located in Mulberry Street (off Norfolk Street).

In 1878, management was handed to Pawson and Brailsford's sons who built new premises in 1884, replacing the old shop by the 'stately and elegant pile' of the Parade Buildings (p51). The company survived into the 1970s.

Now Ready, Price 1s. 6d.,
PAWSON AND BRAILSFORD'S
ILLUSTRATED SHEFFIELD GUIDE.
Comprising a POPULAR and INTERESTING
EPITOME OF
THE EARLY HISTORY OF SHEFFIELD,
THE
RISE AND PROGRESS OF THE TOWN;
ACCOUNT OF
THE PUBLIC AND GOVERNING BODIES,
RELIGIOUS EDIFICES, PUBLIC BUILDINGS,
MONUMENTS, SOCIAL, LITERARY AND
EDUCATIONAL INSTITUTIONS, CHARITIES, &c.;
DESCRIPTIONS OF
THE MANUFACTURES OF SHEFFIELD;
SKETCHES OF
SURROUNDING SCENERY, &c., &c.
THE WORK IS
PROFUSELY ILLUSTRATED with ONE HUNDRED FIRST-
CLASS WOOD ENGRAVINGS.
May also be had extra bound in Cloth, 2s. 6d.

Advertisement for the first 'Illustrated Guide' in the 'Sheffield & Rotherham Independent', Tuesday, June 17, 1862

The Illustrations

This new Guide produced by Pawson and Brailsford improved on the older text-only directories by including illustrations of principal buildings and 'manufactories', together with views of the surrounding countryside. In the first editions the illustrations used wood-engraving, a technique pioneered at the end of the 18th century by artists such as Thomas Bewick (1753–1828). Many illustrated books, such as Ebenezer Rhodes' 'Peak Scenery' (1818-1824) and 'Yorkshire Scenery' (1826) had used copper or steel engravings which produced a much finer level of detail and tone, but had to be printed separately from the text of the book and then added during the binding. Earlier books had used 'wood cuts' which were relatively crude and had a limited useful life. Wood engravings in contrast produced a fine level of detail, could be included alongside conventional printing, and were capable of use and re-use in substantial print runs. Combined with Electrotype, developed in the mid-19th century, the life of the original wood engraving could be extended and many copies of the original block could be made.

A note in the 1862 Guide concerning the illustration of Endcliffe Woods (p112) describes it as having been drawn 'on the wood' (i.e. directly onto the wood engraving block) by Walter Nicholson, a local artist. The image may then have been engraved by an employee of Pawson and Brailsford. Only rarely would the engraver be identified by name.

The second edition of the Illustrated Guide, in 1879, re-used many of the printing blocks seen in the 1862 version, adding and updating others. Further editions in 1889 and 1899 continued the process, and in 1899 added half-tone plates based on photographs, as well as what appear to be photographic reproductions of more detailed line drawings or engravings.

Though Pawson and Brailsford employed their own artists and engravers, several of the illustrations had previously appeared in works from other publishers. For example, the illustration of the Mechanics' Institute (p47) had previously appeared in the 'Sheffield and Rotherham Independent' newspaper on 17th July 1847 while the building was still being built. Several of the illustrations are also found in other guides, including 'Sheffield and its Neighbourhood – Photographically Illustrated' by Theophilus Smith, 1865, which included eleven engravings as chapter end-pieces, along with sixteen photographs, and descriptive text not unlike the 1862 Pawson and Brailsford Guide. Ten of the engravings later appeared in the 1879 Illustrated Guide. The illustration of the Beauchief Abbey Altar-piece (p115), seen in Smith's book and the 1879 Guide, was also included in 'Historical Memorials of Beauchief Abbey' by Sidney Oldall Addy, 1878, with the footnote that 'the engraving … was kindly lent me by Theophilus Smith, Esq., of Sheffield'. Theophilus Smith (1838-1881), described himself as a 'sculptor, designer and photographer'. His grandfather, James, had been an engraver, and his father, Edwin, ran the Cemetery Road Marble and Stone Works together with his son. Edwin's works included the obelisk memorial to Sir Francis Chantrey at Norton (p19).

Beyond Sheffield, the illustrations of Chatsworth, Edensor and Haddon (pp128ff) which first appear in the 1879 Sheffield Guide, are among the splendid sets of illustrations found in Guides to Chatsworth and Haddon published in 1871 & 1872 by Samuel Carter Hall and Llewellynn Jewitt. Llewellynn Frederick William Jewitt (1816-86) was an illustrator and engraver as well as a noted antiquary, and his brother, Thomas Orlando Sheldon Jewitt, was also an engraver.

Though a few of the Hall and Jewitt's Haddon illustrations were signed by Jewitt himself, they were not among those used in the Sheffield Guides. Several of their Chatsworth illustrations were signed W. H. J. Boot, including that of the bridge shown on p129 in this book. It was noted in the Chatsworth guide that some of the illustrations were engraved from photographs by Mr. J. Clarke, but it is not clear whether they include those used in the Sheffield Guides. The engraving of Edensor (p130) was noted as having been taken from a photograph by Mr. E. F. Bampton of Edensor.

The Chatsworth and Haddon Guides, plus a guide to Hardwick Hall including the illustrations on p127, were reprinted in modified form in 'Series 1' of 'The Stately Homes of England' in 1874, also written by Hall and Jewitt. 'Series 2' in 1877 included a guide to Welbeck Abbey with the illustration also used in the Sheffield Guides (p126). The articles had also appeared in 'The Art Journal' edited by Hall between 1839 and 1880.

A number of the industrial illustrations were also included in the 'Official Illustrated Guide to the Great Northern Railway' by George Measom, 1861. As well as producing various railway guides, Measom was himself an engraver, and the engravings in his guide to the Brighton and South Coast Railways were 'by George Measom, from drawings by T. Sulman'. It is therefore possible that the illustrations common to the Sheffield Guides and Measom's Great Northern Guide may also be by Measom and Sulman. They do not however include the illustration of Joseph Rodgers' works (shown on p90) 'signed' by Sulman (see notes on p10 re Sulman).

It is not known whether any of the printing blocks or plates used in the Guides still survive, though the illustration of Thomas Jowitt's Scotia Steel Works (p75) was also used as a frontispiece in the 1976 book 'Sheffield Steel' by K C Barraclough, and was reproduced from a 'block kindly loaned by Frank Smith, Esq.'.

Rather than the lists of individuals and businesses given in the Directories, the Guides provided a narrative of the history of the town, moving on to a description of the institutions and buildings, then of the main manufacturers, and finally of the surrounding area. The narrative description was then followed by advertisements, largely for the major manufacturers, but also for smaller concerns, professionals and tradesmen. These included a number of illustrations, also using wood engravings, and quite a few pages advertising the services of Pawson and Brailsford themselves!

Artists and Engravers

As mentioned earlier, some of the illustrations were drawn 'on the wood' by the original artist, but many would have been copied from original drawings or paintings; from photographs as noted above; or in some cases from earlier illustrations such as the Buck engraving seen at the head of this Preface. In some cases the original artists are mentioned in the text of the Guides or in the captions, and in a few cases within the illustration itself. The engraver who then produced the printing block is also occasionally credited within the body of the illustration.

Theophilus Smith's Photographic Guide (noted above) gives a list of the engravings used and lists the original artists.

Many of the original artists were local and also produced oil and watercolour paintings of Sheffield, often of the same subjects and even of the same view – some of these can be found in public collections and other publications.

The artists and engravers which can be identified are listed below. [TS] indicates that the illustration and artist are listed by Theophilus Smith; [PCF] indicates that the painting is included in the Public Catalogue Foundation and can be seen on the BBC 'Your Paintings' web-site; references of the form [MS X9999.999] relate to accession numbers in the Museums Sheffield collections

> **W. J. Allen** ? – possibly an artist and photographer of that name of Bridge Street, Mansfield.
> > **Darfield Church** (p118) - the artist's name can be seen in the illustration, but is indistinct.
>
> **James Walsham Baldock** (1822-1898) – An artist based in Worksop, Baldock was a founder member of the Sheffield Society of Artists. He was a nephew-in-law of Theophilus Smith.
> > **Upper Room at Manor Lodge** (p106) [TS] – apart from the figures, the view shown closely resembles an etching by William Ibbitt, dated ~1850, now in the Museums Sheffield collection [MS K1913.154].
> > **Altar-piece from Beauchief Abbey** (p115) [TS].
>
> **Edward Blore** (1787-1879) – Blore was an artist and engraver specializing in landscape and architectural subjects. In the 1820s he became an architect, and was involved in completing the design for Buckingham Palace. He drew several illustrations in Hunter's 'Hallamshire' (1819) including the Shrewsbury Chapel in the Parish Church. Charles Askey's engraving from the drawing was the basis of the illustration used in the Guides.
> > **Shrewsbury Chapel** (p15) – the wood engraving is signed H. Dudley (see below).
>
> **William Henry James Boot** (1848-1918) – W. H. J. Boot, named in several illustrations in Jewitt's Chatsworth Guide, worked primarily in oil and watercolour. He was born in Manchester and lived in London, but is known to have exhibited in Sheffield (e.g. in April 1882). His illustrations also appeared in the 'Illustrated London News'.
> > **The Bridge at Chatsworth** (p129).
>
> **William Botham** (active 1802-1834) – Botham was born at Ollerton, Nottinghamshire, was apprenticed as a carver and gilder, and worked with Sir Francis Chantrey. He was an exhibitor at the Royal Academy, and was based in Nottingham and London.
> > **Old House in Townhead Street** (p40) [TS] – a watercolour of the same scene by Botham (dated 1802) is now in a private collection – a copy was included in the book 'The Great Sheffield Picture Show' by David Bostwick (1989). A series of similar watercolours are in the Museums Sheffield Collection (e.g. 'Lady's Bridge' 1802 [MS K1919.98]).

H. Dudley - an engraver also known for his 'Views of the Great Sheffield Flood', some of which can be seen on the Picture Sheffield web-site. A number of these prints are in the Museums Sheffield Collection [MS K1932.18a-l & K1933.20a-t]. Probably **Howard Dudley** (1820-1864), a self-taught wood engraver, who published his first book illustrated with his own engravings when only 14 years old. Dudley died in July 1864, only four months after the Sheffield Flood.

> **Shrewsbury Chapel** (p15) – based on the engraving by Charles Askey found in Hunter's 'Hallamshire' (1819) from a drawing by Edward Blore (see above)
> **Congregational Church, The Wicker** (p22).
> **Armour Plate Rolling** (p69).
> **Wentworth House** (p125) – engraved by H. Dudley from a drawing by Walter Nicholson (see below).

William Ibbitt (1804-1869) – Ibbitt's works include a number of engravings which can be seen on the Picture Sheffield web-site – e.g. 'South-east View of Sheffield from Park Hill', 1855, ref. S11499.

> **Redmires** (p119).
> **Stanedge** (p119).
> **Wharncliffe Crags and Dragon's Den** (p122).
> **Wharncliffe from the Table Rock** (p122).

Walter Nicholson (~1835-1902) – Born in Woodhouse, Nicholson studied at the Sheffield School of Design from 1850, and won many prizes. His working life was spent teaching art and as a landscape painter. His works in the Museums Sheffield collection include several drawings of the aftermath of the Great Sheffield Flood.

> **Endcliffe Wood and Dam** (p112).
> **View of Endcliffe Wood** (p112) – a different view of Endcliffe Woods by Nicholson is seen in a watercolour in the Museums Sheffield Collection [MS K1931.51].
> **Porter Falls** (p119).
> **Upper Room at Carbrook Hall** (p114).
> **Wentworth House** (p125) engraved by H. Dudley (see above).

William James Palmer (active 1858-1896) - known for the engravings in 'The Poets of the Elizabethan Age' published in 1862. Palmer also wrote a guide to the Tyne and its tributaries (1882) containing over 100 engravings by the author.

> **Saw Grinder at Work** (p80) from a drawing by E. Smith (see below).

John Fenney Parkin (1799-1879) – In various directory and other records, John Fenney Parkin was described as an Engraver and Printer rather than an artist. He lived in Sheffield and died in 1879 at his home in Machon Bank, Nether Edge. The Museums Sheffield collection includes a number of his prints and the associated printing plates.

> **Vault under Shrewsbury Chapel** (p15) [TS – listed as 'from a drawing by J. F. Parkin']

Miss Shore – possibly related to the Shore family of Norton Hall.

> **Chantrey's Birth-place** (p115) [TS].

E. Smith - possible Edwin Smith, father of Theophilus Smith.

> **Saw Grinder at Work** (p80) [TS] engraved by W. J. Palmer (see above)
> **Iron and Steel – Crude and Manufactured** (p56) [TS].

Thomas Sulman (~1834-1900) – Sulman was an architectural draughtsman who specialized in using balloons to produce bird's-eye views of cities, including London and New York, for publications such as the Illustrated London News (see Sulman's entry in Wikipedia). He was a London based artist, and it is possible that his illustration of Joseph Rodgers' Works was a commercial commission. Given similarities of style as well as the bird's-eye viewpoint, it is possible that other illustrations may be by the same artist.

> **Joseph Rodgers and Son, Norfolk Street** (p90).

Christopher Thomson (1799 -1871) – Born in Kingston-upon-Hull, Thomson spent time as a sailor, and worked for many years as a house painter. Following an accident in 1851, soon after he moved to Sheffield, he became a professional artist. He was Founder President of the Society for the Promotion of Fine Arts in Sheffield, and Manager and Vice-President of the Mechanics' Institute. He produced many watercolours and oil paintings of the area, as well as a number of volumes of 'The Hallamshire Scrap Book – Views of Hallamshire, Derbyshire, Notts. and Adjoining Counties' containing lithographic plates 'drawn on stone from nature'.

> **Montgomery's Shop and Offices, Hartshead** (p40) – also seen in an Oil Painting by Thomson, dated 1859, in the Museums Sheffield collection [MS K1934.28] [PCF], and as a lithograph in 'The Hallamshire Scrap Book' Part 3, page 4 [MS X1975.916(4)].
> **Shirecliffe** (p118).
> **View of the Rivelin** (p120) – a very similar view is seen in Thomson's painting 'Rivelin Valley near Black Brook', dated 1866, in the Museums Sheffield collection [MS K1912.1] [PCF].
> **View on the Ribbledin** (p120) – a different view of the Ribbledin by Thomson is seen in 'The Hallamshire Scrap Book' Part 2, page 7 [MS X1975.915(7)].
> **Wyming Brook** (p121).

Reprints

The 1862 edition of the Illustrated Guide was reprinted in 1971 in hardback by S. R. Publishers of Wakefield, with a Foreword by Mary Walton, and in paperback in 1985 by Amethyst Press - copies can be found second-hand and in libraries. Copies of the original volumes are more difficult to come by. Editions are occasionally seen on book sellers lists, usually for £100-£200. The 1879 edition, the only edition edited by a named individual, John Taylor, is the most common. That edition is also available in various digital formats in the Internet Archive (archive.org). Searchable PDF downloads of the 1862 and 1879 editions are available from the British Library (www.bl.uk) and printed British Library reprints are available through online book-sellers. An abridged reprint of the 1879 edition has also been published recently (in 2013) by ACMRetro (www.acmretro.com) in Sheffield.

This volume

The project to produce this volume came about while searching for mid 19th century illustrations to use on the covers for two previous publications ('The Tour of the Don', Volumes 1 and 2, 2013). The quality of the illustrations in the Guides suggested that they deserved a wider audience, and the detail they contained provided fascinating glimpses into 19th century life, fashions and transport, as well as showing the development of the town centre and the growth of the local industry. The aim of this volume was not to produce another reprint of the original Guide, but rather to bring together illustrations from the different Guides to provide a pictorial summary of the town and area, and where possible to place them into context. The selection of illustrations has been driven by the available images and is therefore inevitably incomplete, ignoring much of the town, and many of the town's products and producers. This volume does not attempt to cover the narrative or the advertisements included in the guides.

To provide the context for the images, brief descriptive notes have been added, based in part on the text of the Guides, but including other information, particularly where the building has since disappeared or has changed significantly, and some trivia unearthed during the research. These notes also provide a reference back to the original Guides giving the volume(s) and page(s) where the image can be found. These have the form [1879 p1, 1889 p1, 1899 p1] (this being the reference for the above 'View of Sheffield').

The half-tone photographs found in the 1899 edition have not been included due to the limited quality of their reproduction.

The advertising seen in the Guides has not been included in this volume, though this also includes some excellent illustrations, as well as insights into life in the 19th century. Perhaps that is the subject of another book!

Page decorations, such as that seen below, have been taken from the 1879 Guide. The coats of arms seen on the Contents and Acknowledgement pages are taken from the 1879 and 1899 Guides.

Churches

ST. PAUL'S CHURCH.

PARISH CHURCH, SHEFFIELD.

The main body of the Parish Church seen here in 1862 was probably built in about 1430, though its foundations are thought to date back as far as the 12th century. By 1862 the addition of chapels, side aisles and vestries had changed what had been a cruciform layout to a rectangular ground plan.

Originally dedicated to St. Peter, in the reformation it's designation was changed to 'Holy Trinity'. It was renamed again in the 19th century, and since 1914 it has been 'The Cathedral Church of St. Peter and St. Paul'.

The premises of Pawson & Brailsford (on the right of the above picture) were replaced by the Parade Buildings (p51) in 1885. The gateway shown was replaced in 1890 and the replacement piers can now be seen to the east of the church.

The church has undergone many changes over the centuries, and in changes made in 1867 the clock was moved from the south wall (as seen above) to the tower (seen on the 1879 view on the right). In 1880, new transepts were added.

Burials in the church-yard ended in 1855 following the opening of the Anglican section of the General Cemetery in 1850. Graves were then cleared in schemes to widen Campo Lane and Church Street. The most recent scheme, in the 1990s, was during the building of the Supertram.

In the 20th century, major extensions were made on the north (Campo Lane) side of the building, and a new west-end and lantern tower were added in the 1960s.

[1862 p35] & [1879 p69, 1889 p36]

PARISH CHURCH, SHEFFIELD.

THE SHREWSBURY CHAPEL.—FROM AN ENGRAVING IN HUNTER'S HALLAMSHIRE.

The Shrewsbury Chapel stands in the south-east angle of the building. It was added to the Parish Church in the reign of Henry VIII (~1520) by George Talbot, the 4th Earl of Shrewsbury, and until 1933 was technically a Catholic chapel, belonging to the Duke of Norfolk, in an Anglican church.

The monument seen in the archway on the left is that of the 4th Earl and his wives. The elaborate monument seen on the south wall through the pointed arch is that of the 6th Earl, and omits any mention of his wife, 'Bess of Hardwick'.

The screen seen here was moved to the North Transept in 1933.

The vault below the Shrewsbury Chapel was described by Joseph Hunter in his 'Hallamshire' (1819, p150) from a visit made in 1809, listing 17 people who were buried there between 1520 and 1787. By then only two coffins could be seen, those of Gilbert the 7th Earl (d. 1616), and Henry Howard (d. 1787), a descendant of the family.

In 1858, the vault was again opened, and the walls and floor were excavated. Three more bodies and some loose bones were found under the floor, one body was unnamed, and the other two were unrelated to Hunter's list. It was investigated again in 2013, but no more bodies were found.

[1862 p37, 1879 p71, 1889 p38, 1899 p55] &
[1879 p74, 1889 p39, 1899 p57]

VAULT UNDER SHREWSBURY CHAPEL AS OPENED IN 1858.

ST. PAUL'S CHURCH.

The building of St. Paul's Church started in 1719, but, due to a dispute about the appointment of a minister, it was not opened until 1740. The 'New Church' can be seen on the left of the 1740/45 'View of Sheffield' shown in the Preface (p5). The original of that engraving clearly shows the tower without its dome, which was not added until 1769.

The church was demolished in 1938 and the site is now the Peace Gardens next to the Town Hall.

[1862 p42, 1879 p77]

As the town expanded more churches were built within the extensive parish. St. Paul's (above) and St. James' (p29) had been built in the town centre by 1789, and in the 1820s four more churches were built in Attercliffe (Christ Church), Shalesmoor (St. Philip's), Bramall Lane (St. Mary's) and Portobello (St. George's) funded in part by the 'Million Act' of 1818. This Act allocated a million pounds to fund church building in celebration of the victory at Waterloo.

St. George's is no longer used as a church, and is now part of Sheffield University.

[1879 p79]

ST. GEORGE'S CHURCH.

ECCLESALL CHURCH.

The chapel which predated Ecclesall Church was built in about 1406, with services being taken by the monks of Beauchief Abbey. The services ended at the dissolution of the abbey in 1536 and were not restored until 1622. The church shown here was built in 1788, improved in 1843, and enlarged in 1864. Until 1845, Ecclesall was part of the Parish of Sheffield, the church being a 'Chapel of Ease'. In 1845, the single parish was subdivided into 25 separate parishes, including Ecclesall.

Since the publication of the Guides, Ecclesall Church has been further extended and reordered in 1907, 1964 and 1997.

[1879 p78, 1889 p41]

The original St. Mark's, not pictured in the Guides, was known as the 'Iron Church'. It was a temporary construction built in 1859 to serve the expanding suburbs of Broomhall and Broomhill. The stone building shown here replaced it in 1871, and the iron church was moved to Carbrook. It stood as St. Bartholemew's, Carbrook, until replaced by a stone building consecrated in 1891.

St. Mark's was largely destroyed by an incendiary dropped in the Sheffield Blitz in December 1940 leaving only the tower and spire intact. The new body of the church that exists today was built between 1958 and 1963.

[1879 p85, 1889 p45, 1899 p64]

ST. MARK'S CHURCH, BROOMFIELD.

The parish of Ranmoor was created in the prosperous suburbs to the west of Sheffield in 1877, and the Church of St. John the Evangelist shown here was a gift from John Newton Mappin. It was opened on 24th April 1879.

The church was largely destroyed by fire in January 1887, with only the tower and spire surviving. At 200 ft. (61 m.) it was, and remains, the tallest spire in Sheffield.

THE CHURCH OF ST. JOHN THE EVANGELIST, RANMOOR.

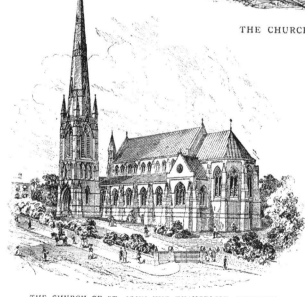

THE CHURCH OF ST. JOHN THE EVANGELIST, RANMOOR.

The church was rebuilt on a modified design by the same architect, E. M. Gibbs of Flockton and Gibbs. The building as it now stands, and as shown on the left in a view from the 1889 Guide, was reopened in September 1888.

The interior was reordered in 1991, in a way which the Pevsner Guide describes as 'incomprehensibly unsympathetic'.

[1879 p303] & [1889 p46]

THE CHURCH OF ST. JOHN THE EVANGELIST, ABBEYDALE.

St. John's Church, Abbeydale, and St. James' at Norton were both built beyond the Sheffield boundary in Derbyshire.

St John's was built at the expense of Mr. John Roberts of Abbeydale Hall. It was opened in 1876, four years after the nearby Dore and Totley Station.

The original building, shown here, can still be recognised behind the later modifications.

The neighbouring Church Rooms were added in 1893, and were used as a V.A.D. Hospital in WW1 – they are now a Post Office Sorting Office.

[1879 p328]

Though a church may have existed in Norton in the Saxon period, the present building dates from the 11th century. It is dedicated to St. James the Great.

Norton was the birth place of the sculptor, Sir Francis Chantrey (p115), and after his death a memorial obelisk was erected in 1854 on what was known as Norton Green. The obelisk, seen in the foreground, was made from a single block of 'Cheesewiring Granite' from Cornwall, by Edwin Smith, the father of Theophilus Smith (p7).

Norton village became part of Sheffield in two stages in 1901 and 1933.

[1862 p195, 1879 p326, 1889 p198]

NORTON CHURCH AND CHANTREY'S MONUMENT.

ST. THOMAS' CHURCH, WINCOBANK.

The community of Wincobank grew rapidly in the 1860s and '70s due to the development of the Yorkshire Engine Works of J. Crowley & Co.

St. Thomas' Church was opened in 1876 to serve the new parish which then had a population of over 4,000.

The church is now part of the combined parish of Brightside and Wincobank, and continues in its original role, with very few external changes.

[1879 p87]

St. Marie's Roman Catholic Church was built between 1846 and 1850. It replaced a chapel opened in 1816, which had itself replaced the Catholic meeting room behind 'The Lord's House' (i.e. The Duke of Norfolk's House) in Fargate.

In 1902 a new presbytery was added, and the church was reordered in the 1970s and again in 2012.

St. Marie's became the Cathedral Church of the new Catholic Diocese of Hallam in 1980.

[1862 p58, 1879 p103]

ST. MARIE'S CHURCH.

BRUNSWICK CHAPEL.

Brunswick Chapel, opened in 1834, was one of the three chapels, along with Norfolk Street and Park, in the newly formed Wesleyan Methodist East Circuit of Sheffield. It stood in South Street (renamed the Moor in 1922) on Sheffield Moor (the area now better known as Moorfoot).

The chapel was damaged in the Blitz of 1940, and was demolished in 1956. The site is now under a dual carriageway (St. Mary's Gate).

St. Mary's Church, Bramall Lane, can be seen in the background.

[1862 p49, 1879 p91, 1889 p49]

The Hanover Chapel of the United Methodist Free Church was opened at the junction of Broomspring Lane and Hanover Street in 1860. The building was on the edge of the Broomhall Estate which John Watson had laid out as middle-class housing in the 1830s, contrasting with the industry and back-to-back housing found on the Fitzwilliam land towards the town centre.

The 1860 building was demolished in the 1970s and replaced by a smaller, more practical building. This continued as a Methodist Church until 2008 and is now the 'Sheffield Jesus Centre'.

[1862 p51, 1879 p93, 1889 p50]

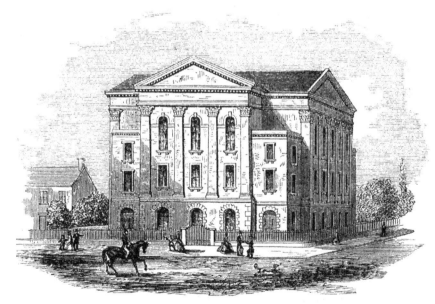

HANOVER STREET CHAPEL.

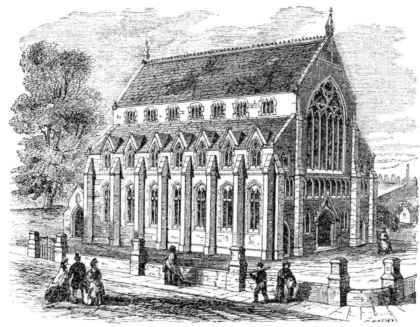

CONGREGATIONAL CHURCH, WICKER.

The Wicker Congregational Church, was built in 1854 at the top of Spital Hill, at its junction with Gower Street. It was one of three churches (here, at Burngreave, and on Queen Street) built to cater for the growing congregation of the Nether Chapel in the town centre.

The three churches reunited with the Nether Chapel in 1971 forming the Central Congregational Church, and this became the Central United Reform Church in 1972.

The Wicker Church was demolished in the late 1960s and the site is now known as Ellesmere Green.

[1862 p53, 1879 p 98]

Cemetery Road Congregational Church opened in 1859, and stood at the junction of Cemetery Road and Summerfield Street.

Its controversial first minister was Rev. Brewin Grant, who in April 1870 moved to the Anglican Church and became an Anglican minister. In the 1879 Guide, the church was said to still be known as 'Brewin Grant's Church'.

The church was demolished in the 1960s to make way for an extension to the Sheffield Twist Drill and Steel Company – this too was demolished in the 1990s and the site is now the car park for a health club.

[1862 p55, 1879 p99, 1889 p51, 1899 p72]

CONGREGATIONAL CHURCH, CEMETERY ROAD.

BAPTIST CHAPEL, CEMETERY ROAD.

The Baptist Church on Cemetery Road, Sharrow, was opened in 1859. It has now been in continuous use as a Baptist Church for over 150 years.

A sunday school and meeting rooms were added to the rear in about 1900 and a new entrance was built more recently, but the distinctive Romanesque styling can still easily be recognized from the 1862 illustration.

[1862 p56]

The Baptist Church in Glossop Road was built between 1869 and 1871, and continued to be used as a church until 1970 when it was converted for use as a theatre.

It is now the University of Sheffield Drama Studio. The conversion created a 200 seat auditorium, three rehearsal studios and other supporting facilities, and a variety of groups now stage over 40 productions each year.

[1879 p101, 1889 p53, 1899 p73]

BAPTIST CHURCH, GLOSSOP-ROAD.

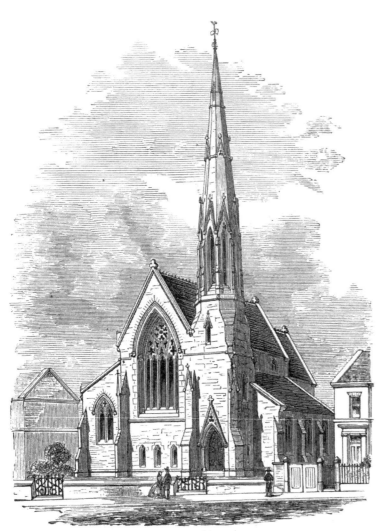

ST. ANDREW'S CHURCH.

St. Andrew's Presbyterian Church came into being in 1853, and the building shown here was opened on Hanover Street (now Upper Hanover Street) in 1856. It was shown on many maps as 'The Scotch Church'.

The roof was destroyed by an incendiary in December 1940, and the church reopened in 1953.

The Presbyterians became part of the United Reform Church in 1972.

The church has been in almost continuous use for over 150 years, and externally the building is little changed from the 1862 illustration.

[1862 p57, 1879 p105, 1889 p55]

Education

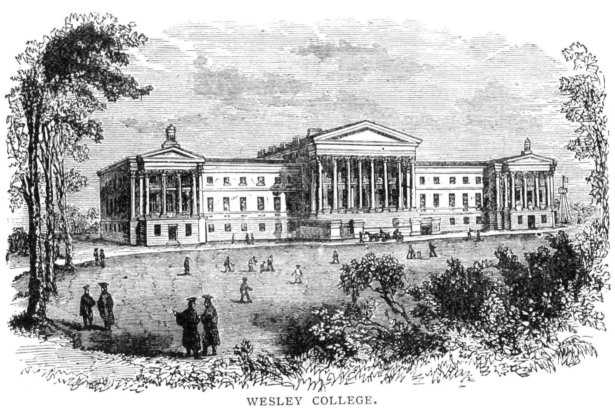

WESLEY COLLEGE.

COLLEGIATE SCHOOL.

The Sheffield Collegiate School was an Anglican institution opened in 1835 in new buildings near the corner of Ecclesall Road and Collegiate Crescent. The view above from the 1879 edition of the Guide shows Ecclesall Road and the gated entrance to the Crescent and to the Broomhall Estate laid out in the 1830s. The lodge still stands at the junction.

In 1884 the school was taken over by the Sheffield Grammar School which moved from St. George's Square (now Mappin Street). The combined school became the Sheffield Royal Grammar School the following year.

The city council merged the school with Wesley College (p27) in 1905 to create the King Edward VII School, and the Collegiate site became the Sheffield Teacher Training College. The main building (shown right) was extended in 1911, though it retained its basic shape.

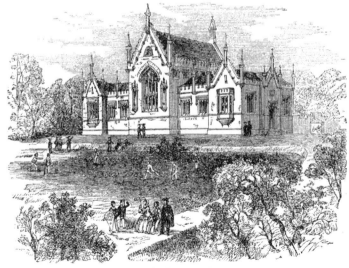

In 1966 the college was renamed as the Sheffield City College of Education. It became part of Sheffield Polytechnic in 1976, and Sheffield Hallam University in 1992.

The name of the Collegiate School lives on in the Sheffield Collegiate Cricket Club.

[1879 p147, 1889 p87] & [1862 p78]

COLLEGIATE SCHOOL.

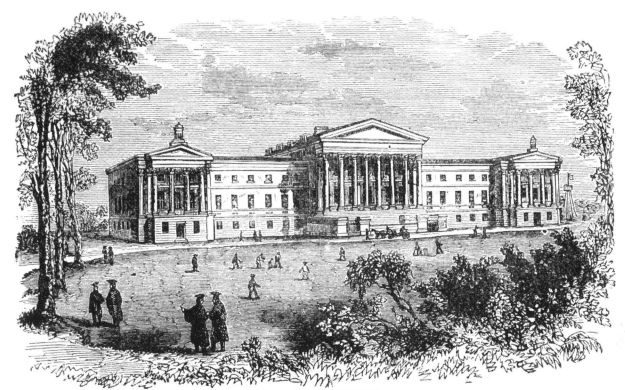

WESLEY COLLEGE.

The 'Wesleyan Proprietary Grammar School' was opened in 1838. All of the shareholders were members of the Wesleyan Methodist Church, in contrast to the Collegiate School the proprietors of which were primarily Anglican. The building as shown here was completed in 1840.

The name was changed to Wesley College in 1844 by a Royal Warrant which constituted it as a college of the University of London.

In 1905 the college was purchased by Sheffield City Council and merged with Sheffield Royal Grammar School (p26) to form King Edward VII School. The interior of the building was redeveloped to provide additional height in the rooms and to remove the dormitories.

The school has recently undergone an extensive refurbishment which included restoration of the series of air raid shelters built under the 'Close' in front of the main building during WW2.

[1879 p149, 1889 p88]

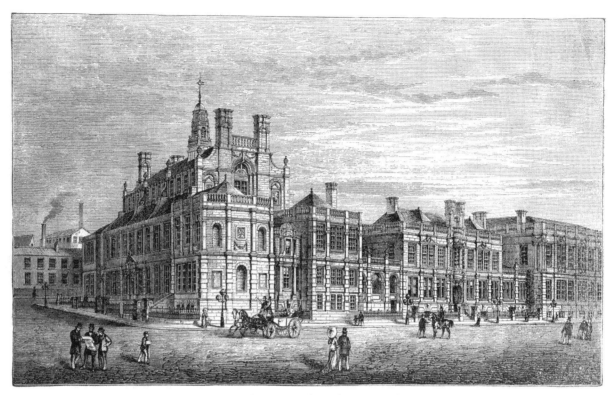

CENTRAL BOARD SCHOOLS AND OFFICES.

In 1870 the first School Board in the country was established in Sheffield. The Central Schools (on the left) and the School Board offices (linking the schools to Firth College on the right) were opened in 1879 along Leopold Street. The new street had been laid out between Barker's Pool and Bow Street (now the lower end of West Street) following the demolition of old houses and works in Smith Street and Sands Paviour.

Firth College was built by Mark Firth, the steel manufacturer, to provide Adult Education and Cambridge University Extension courses teaching arts and science subjects to university level.

In 1897 the college together with the Medical School (p29) and the Technical School in St. George's Square (Mappin Street) received a Royal Charter as 'The University College of Sheffield'. They did not receive full University status until 1905.

Between 1933 and 1964 the college building was used as the Central Technical School before this moved to Stradbroke as The City School.

In 2001 the remaining City Education Offices were relocated and the Leopold Street buildings were redeveloped to include apartments and a hotel.

[1879 p157, 1889 p94, 1899 p120] &
[1879 p159, 1889 p96, 1899 p123]

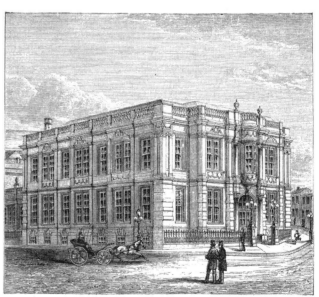

THE FIRTH COLLEGE.

SCHOOL OF MEDICINE.

The Medical School was founded in 1828 at the junction of Surrey Street and Arundel Street (~Arundel Gate). Following the opening of Firth College, the struggling medical school moved to Leopold Street to the building shown here which still stands close to the junction with Church Street, and still carries the school motto 'Ars Longa, Vita Brevis' and the date 1888 over the door.

In 1897 the school became part of 'The University College of Sheffield'.

The church seen on the left is St. James', consecrated in 1789 and destroyed in the Blitz of 1940.

[1889 p91, 1899 p125]

The Sheffield School of Design was established in 1843 in Victoria Street, Glossop Road, and the building shown here was opened in 1857 in Arundel Street (~Arundel Gate).

It was destroyed in WW2, and what was by then the Sheffield College of Arts and Crafts, moved to premises in Psalter Lane.

The college merged with the Colleges of Education and Technology in 1969 to form Sheffield Polytechnic, the predecessor to Sheffield Hallam University.

[1862 p80, 1879 p151, 1889 p90, 1899 p116]

THE SCHOOL OF ART

RANMOOR COLLEGE.

Ranmoor College opened in 1864 to train young men as ministers for the Methodist New Connection.

It later served as a Royal Hospital Nurses Hostel (1917-40) and as Air Raid Precautions Headquarters during the Second World War.

The building was demolished in 1965 after being used for 16 years as a hall of residence for Sheffield University, and the site on Fulwood Road is now occupied by housing association flats

[1879 p154, 1889 p92, 1899 p119]

Workshops for the blind were established in West Street in 1860 to provide instruction and employment. These were created largely due to the efforts of the Misses Harrison of Weston Hall (later the City Museum).

The Sheffield School for the Blind opened on Manchester Road in 1880.

The school closed in 1997 as children were integrated into mainstream schools. For its last forty years it was operated by Sheffield City Council Education Department.

[1879 p169, 1889 p102]

SCHOOL FOR THE BLIND.

CHURCH OF ENGLAND EDUCATIONAL INSTITUTE.

'The Church of England Instruction Society' was established in 1840 in Carver Street and moved to the building shown here in St. James' Street close to the Parish Church in 1860. The building was on the site of the old vicarage.

The 'Institute' taught a wide range of subjects to young working adults, largely as evening classes and almost all were taught by volunteer teachers, mainly local professionals.

By 1911, the building was being used as the Central Board Schools Cookery Department. Later it was the Diocesan Office. In 1981 it was converted to a bar which has had several names, most recently, the 'Church House'.

[1862 p84, 1879 p152]

The first Free Library in Sheffield was created in the Mechanic's Institute in Surrey Street in 1856 (p47), and a number of branch libraries were opened over the next 20 years. Highfield Library, shown here, opened in 1876. The picture does not show St. Barnabas' Church, which stands behind the library and was opened in the same year.

The building is still used as a branch library and was refurbished in 2013.

[1879 p120]

HIGHFIELD BRANCH LIBRARY.

Hospitals and Charities

SHREWSBURY HOSPITAL.

SHREWSBURY HOSPITAL.

The Shrewsbury Hospital is not a hospital in the modern sense.

The charity was founded in 1616 on the death of Gilbert Talbot, the 7th Earl of Shrewsbury, and from 1665 provided a group of almshouses close to the River Sheaf opposite the Castle (now the Park Square roundabout). These were demolished in 1827 and replaced by the buildings shown here.

The 'hospital' still stands in Norfolk Road and the charity continues to provide accommodation for applicants 'of pensionable age'.

[1862 p91, 1879 p165]

The General Infirmary was opened in 1795 in the open countryside of Shalesmoor.

Additions over the next century included an octagonal outpatients department in 1884, and a nurses home in 1897.

It became the Royal Infirmary in 1897, the year of Queen Victoria's visit, and closed in 1980.

The buildings are now used as offices and the grounds include a supermarket and its car park.

[1862 p88, 1879 p161]

SHEFFIELD GENERAL INFIRMARY.

PUBLIC HOSPITAL AND DISPENSARY.

The Public Dispensary was established in Tudor Street in 1832. This soon moved to what had been a private house in West Street, and in 1858 a new building was started, also in West Street.

This new building, shown in this 1862 illustration, was opened in 1860 and included accommodation for 61 in-patients.

[1862 p89]

In 1868 the building was enlarged and the number of beds increased to 105. By 1893, plans were made to replace the hospital, and in 1895 the Sheffield Royal Hospital (shown on p36) was opened, and named by the command of Queen Victoria. The demolition of the old dispensary was completed in 1906.

[1879 p162, 1889 p98]

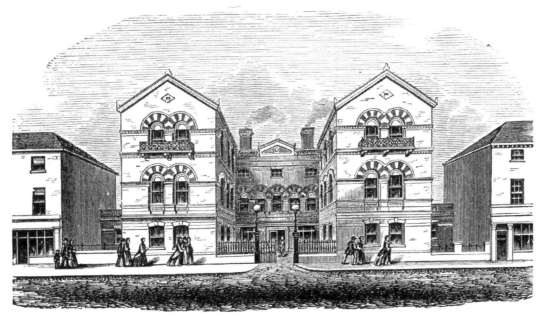

PUBLIC HOSPITAL AND DISPENSARY.

THE JESSOP HOSPITAL FOR WOMEN.

The Sheffield Hospital for Women was established in 1864 in Figtree Lane near to the parish church, and in 1878 moved to a Upper Gell Street. The new hospital was funded by Thomas Jessop, and was named The Jessop Hospital for Women.

The building was enlarged in 1899 and throughout the 20th century, finally closing in 2001 when the maternity unit moved to the new Jessop Wing on Tree Root Walk.

[1879 p163, 1889 p99, 1899 p130]

The Royal Hospital occupied a site fronting onto West Street and bounded by Eldon Street and Westfield Terrace. The hospital replaced the Public Dispensary (p35), and was still under development when opened in 1895. Construction was completed in 1912, though further changes occurred throughout its life.

In 1939, the Royal Hospital merged with the Royal Infirmary to create the Royal Sheffield Infirmary and Hospital, and with the creation of the National Health Service in 1948, the United Sheffield Hospitals.

The hospital was closed and demolished in 1978.

[1899 p129]

SHEFFIELD ROYAL HOSPITAL.

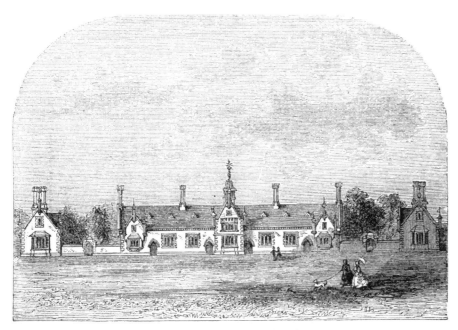

LICENSED VICTUALLERS' ASYLUM

The Sheffield & Rotherham Licensed Victuallers' Society provided an institution for the support of its members and their widows.

The buildings shown in the 1862 illustration (left) were at Grimesthorpe and date from 1848. They overlooked the Midland Railway, and were set in an area of open fields and scattered houses.

The outer blocks seen in the illustration are not seen in maps of the time, though they may have been included in the plans.

The original asylum soon became surrounded by factories, and a new building was erected in 1878 opposite the Dore & Totley Railway Station at Abbeydale.

The old houses at Grimesthorpe became numbers 11 to 17 Lincoln Place, and survived until about 1967. The site, between Bland Street and Carlisle Street is now a demolition yard.

The Abbeydale almshouses are now known as Woodland View and the central hall is used as a masonic hall.

[1862 p93] & [1879 p167, 1889 p101, 1899 p133]

THE LICENSED VICTUALLERS' ASYLUM.

The Town Centre

VIEW OF FARGATE.

OLD HOUSE IN TOWNHEAD-STREET, BUILT IN 1680.

The illustration of these old houses is based on an 1802 watercolour, 'Little Hill at the top of Campo Lane' by W. Botham (now in a private collection).

The 'Crofts', the area between Townhead Street and Lee Croft, had developed as the town expanded across the open fields (the crofts). By the 1860s this was a slum area with the highest death rates in Sheffield. Between 1898 and 1907 the area was redeveloped and included the Hawley Street flats, the first council rented housing in Sheffield.

[1879 p6, 1889 p3, 1899 p3]

At the start of the 19th century, in Hartshead, at the opposite end of Campo Lane from Townhead Street, stood the offices of the 'Sheffield Iris' newspaper, managed by the poet James Montgomery. By 1862, the shop and offices had become a beer-house known as the 'Montgomery Tavern' – the name can be seen in window facing the viewer.

An oil painting dated 1859 showing this view towards Campo Lane by the same artist, Christopher Thomson (1799-1871), is in the Museums Sheffield collection.

[1862 p104, 1879 p194, 1889 p118, 1899 p158]

MONTGOMERY'S SHOP AND OFFICE, HARTSHEAD, FROM A SKETCH BY MR. C. THOMSON.

THE WHOLESALE VEGETABLE MARKET AND EXTERIOR VIEW OF NORFOLK MARKET HALL.

The Norfolk Market Hall was opened in 1851 and stretched between Castlefolds Market (seen in the foreground) and the Haymarket. It occupied the site of the former Tontine Inn.

The market hall was 296 feet long, 115 feet wide and 45 feet high in the centre. It provided accommodation for 45 shops and 56 stalls. The roof was made of iron and glass, and in the centre of the building there was a fountain made from green moonstone in an Italian design.

The market was demolished in 1959, to be replaced by a Woolworth's store, and later by Wilkinsons.

The above view is along Exchange Street toward the Old Town Hall, the clock tower of which can be seen in the distance. This was later redesigned and became the Crown Court. Since 1997 the building has been unused.

[1862 p65] &
[1862 p64, 1879 p141]

INTERIOR OF THE NORFOLK MARKET HALL.

WEST FRONT VIEW OF THE SHAMBLES, WITH POST OFFICE AND ELLIOTT'S MONUMENT.

The Shambles, also known as the Fitzalan Market, were built on the site of the old medieval market cross in 1786 to sell meat, fish, vegetables, and other goods. They were redesigned in 1856.

The Post Office occupied the west end of the new building and looked out across the old Market Place (Angel Street) to a memorial to Ebenezer Elliott, the 'Corn Law Rhymer' who died in 1849. The memorial was moved to Weston Park in 1875.

The Post Office was replaced in 1871 by a new building at the top of the Haymarket, now the Yorkshire Bank.

[1862 p67]

The east end of the Shambles, facing onto the Haymarket, housed the Electric Telegraph Company Offices, and also the Fitzalan Public House.

The building was demolished in 1930, and in 1932 'C&A Modes' was built on the site. 8 years later this was destroyed in the Sheffield Blitz. The site was re-developed by C&A, and later became a Primark store.

[1862 p66]

EAST FRONT OF SHAMBLES, WITH OFFICES OF ELECTRIC TELEGRAPH COMPANY, ETC.

NEW CORN EXCHANGE.

In 1830 the open air corn market was replaced by the 'Old' Corn Exchange located to the east of the River Sheaf on the former site of the old Shrewsbury Hospital (p34). This was replaced in 1881 by the 'New' Corn Exchange shown here. The new exchange stood to the west of the Norfolk Market Hall and Castlefolds Market. This view, facing east, includes St. John's Church, Park Hill, in the distance.

The central hall was destroyed by a fire in 1947 and the remainder was demolished in 1964. The site is now under Park Square Roundabout.

[1879 p143, 1889 p84, 1899 p109]

The offices of the Sheffield United Gas Light Company in Commercial Street were built in 1874 and stood next to the new General Post Office (to the left of the illustration).

The Gas Board offices were closed in 1972, and there have been several attempts to have the building demolished. It is now Grade II* listed and the outside remains largely as it did in 1879.

[1879 p115, 1889 p64, 1899 p82]

THE GAS COMPANY'S OFFICES, COMMERCIAL-STREET.

THE HALLAMSHIRE SAVINGS BANK.

The Sheffield & Hallamshire Savings Bank was established in 1819, largely due the efforts of James Montgomery. The bank operated from the Cutlers' Hall until 1832 when the hall was rebuilt, and then from premises in Surrey Street. The building shown here was opened in Norfolk Street in 1860.

In 1976 the bank became part of TSB.

The building remains externally almost unchanged, and is now the 'Old Monk' public house.

[1862 p94, 1879 p113, 1889 p61]

The Sheffield & Hallamshire Bank built their head office at 17 Church Street in 1838.

The building was enlarged in 1878, and became part of the Midland Bank in 1913. Prior to the merger, the bank had been one of the last independent banks in England.

In 1992 Midland became a member of the HSBC Group. The branch closed in 2008 and the building has been converted into retail units including a Tesco Express.

[1879 p112, 1889 p59]

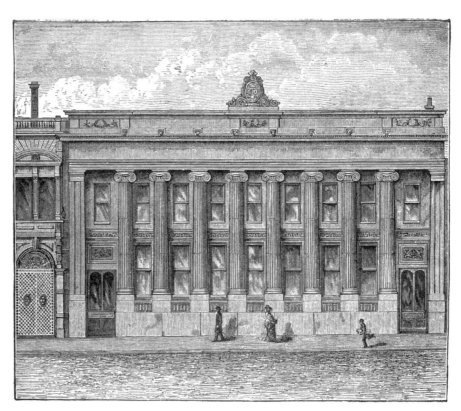

THE SHEFFIELD AND HALLAMSHIRE BANK.

BIRMINGHAM, DISTRICT AND COUNTIES BANK.

The London and Northern Bank opened a Sheffield branch in Old Haymarket in 1864. The branch is noted but not illustrated in the 1879 Guide.

Following a series of mergers, the company became the Midland Banking Co. and the branch moved to new premises (shown here) built in Fitzalan Square on the site of the Kings Arms Hotel. The new branch opened in 1881.

The new branch stood on the corner of Fitzalan Square across Commercial Street from the new Post Office built in 1871 (now the Yorkshire Bank standing at the top of Haymarket).

Through the 1880s the name of the bank changed several times and by 1889, the date of the illustration, the bank had become the Birmingham, District and Counties Bank

By 1909 the name seen on the branch had again changed to the United Counties Bank, and in 1916 it became a branch of Barclays Bank.

The branch moved to 14, Commercial Street in 1969 and the old building was demolished to allow the widening of Commercial Street. The remainder of the site is now occupied by shops including a branch of Cooplands.

[1889 p60]

THE YORKSHIRE PENNY BANK.

The West Riding Penny Savings Bank was established in Leeds in 1859, though its name soon changed to the Yorkshire Penny Bank as it extended its operation into the rest of the county.

In 1889 the Sheffield branch of the Yorkshire Penny Bank occupied the ground floor of the newly erected building shown in this illustration, on the corner of Fargate and Surrey Street. The bank became Yorkshire Bank in 1959, and a branch continues to operate from the building.

The building also included the Albany Hotel and Restaurant, run by the Sheffield Café Company. This was later also known as the Albany Temperance Hotel.

The view down Surrey Street on the right includes the former Mechanics' Institute, which by 1889 was used as the Council Hall and Free Library (p47). Beyond it is the site of the present Central Library.

[1889 p62]

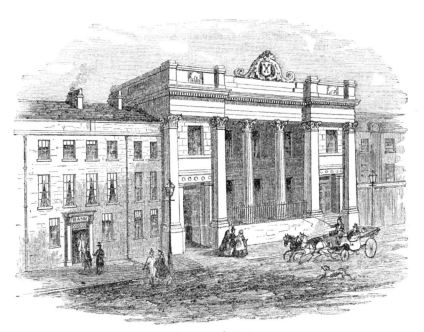

THE CUTLERS' HALL.

The Cutlers' Hall which still stands on Church Street is the third such building on the site. The first was built in 1638 and replaced in 1725. The third building, shown here, was built in 1832. The arms above the portico are those of the London Cutlers – the Arms of the Hallamshire Cutlers (p4) were not granted until 1875.

In 1867, the building was extended by adding a Banqueting Hall to the rear, and in 1888 the frontage was extended to the west, as can be seen in the view of Church Street on p52.

An attic storey was added in 1928, altering the roof line.

[1862 p62]

The Mechanics' Institute was established in 1832 and the building shown here, at the junction of Surrey Street and Tudor Street (now Tudor Square), was erected in 1848 to house the Institute and an 'Athenæum' aimed at providing a social mix between the working and middle classes of the town. The combination failed financially, in part due to the creation of a rival Athenæum (see p48), and in 1851 the original Athenæum became a separate club called the Lyceum which was finally wound-up in 1854.

From 1856 the lower floor was rented to the council for use as the Free Library, and in 1864 the building was purchased by the Town Council and the lecture room became the Council Hall.

The building was demolished in 1931 prior to the building of the new Central Library.

[1862 p83, 1879 p62, 1889 p33]

MECHANICS' INSTITUTE.

The 1879/89 caption for this illustration reads 'Council Hall and Central Free Library'.

THE ATHENÆUM.

The formation of an Athenæum in association with the new Mechanics' Institute (p47) was proposed in January 1847. A split in the support led to the creation of a separate Athenæum in Norfolk Street, specifically aimed at the middle classes of the town. This Athenæum later moved to the corner of George Street, and the building shown here, also in George Street, was purchased in 1859. It included coffee, dining, smoking and chess rooms, a news-room, library and a 'suite of rooms for the use of ladies'.

The building was bombed in 1940, and the site is now occupied by the Cutlers' Hotel.

The name of the club continues in the Sheffield Athenæum Chess club.

[1862 p75]

The Sheffield Club was established in 1843 as a club for the 'elite' of the town. Membership was by ballot and annual fees were 6 guineas (£6.30p), compared to the open membership and fee of 25 shillings (£1.25) at the Athenæum.

In 1862 the club moved to their new premises, see here, at the corner of Norfolk Street & Mulberry Street.

The Club moved to George Street in 1964, and relocated to Tapton Hall in 2000.

[1862 p76, 1879 p118]

THE SHEFFIELD CLUB.

VIEW OF VICTORIA RAILWAY STATION AND HOTEL.

The Sheffield, Ashton-under-Lyne and Manchester Railway was begun in 1838 to link the two sides of the pennines via the Woodhead Tunnel. The line reached Sheffield in 1845 and terminated at Bridgehouses, close to Nursery Street and what is now Derek Dooley Way. Two years later the company amalgamated with two other lines to form the Manchester, Sheffield & Lincolnshire Railway, the line was extended beyond its previous terminus at Bridgehouses and the Victoria Station was opened in 1851.

The hotel was opened next to the station in 1862 by the Sheffield Hotel Company, and received its 'Royal' prefix in 1875 when it was visited by the Prince and Princess of Wales who came to Sheffield to open the newly created Firth Park (p111).

A new station frontage was added in 1908, and further improvements were made in the 1930s. The last passenger service operated in 1970, and the station buildings were demolished in 1989. They were replaced by a car park and an extension to the hotel, now the 'Holiday Inn Royal Victoria Sheffield'.

[1862 p97]

THE CRIMEAN MONUMENT AND VIEW OF MOOR HEAD, ETC.

Sheffield Moor Head stood at the junction of Furnival Street (now Furnival Gate) and South Street (now The Moor). This view from the 1862 Guide shows Moor Head facing south-west along South Street from what would now be the bottom of Pinstone Street.

The illustration shows the Crimea Monument which was completed in 1863. The 58 ft. (17.7 m.) granite monument was topped by a 10 ft. (3 m.) statue of Queen Victoria representing 'Honour'.

The area was redeveloped in 1957 and the statue was moved to the Botanical Gardens where it stood until 2004. The statue was not thought to fit with the original design of the gardens and was removed with a view to placing it in Barkers Pool as part of the new Retail Quarter. It is thought to be in storage in a council depot, and as with the promised Retail Quarter, its ultimate fate is unknown. The fate of the column is also unclear – the sections were used in a children's playground in Upperthorpe.

The stone griffins which sat on the top of the square base of the monument were used to produce moulds for the bronze griffins placed in Castle Square in 1995.

[1862 p71]

VIEW OF HIGH STREET.

This above view of the High Street shows the results of the widening, completed in 1895, during which the south side of the street was demolished and entirely redeveloped. The new buildings included the 'Foster's' Building seen on the right on the corner of Fargate, the upper stories and roof-line of which can still be recognized above the modern shop frontages. This building included the first American 'elevator' in Sheffield.

On the left stand the Parade Buildings (or Parade Chambers), completed in 1885 for Pawson & Brailsford, publishers of the Illustrated Guides. This replaced the old shop seen on p14.

The first floor of Parade Buildings was occupied by the Sheffield Stock Exchange which moved to the top of the Haymarket (formerly the head post office and now a Yorkshire Bank) in 1911. It continued to operate until 1967 when the creation of British Steel reduced the need for a local exchange largely dealing in steel makers stocks.

[1899 p34]

VIEW OF CHURCH STREET.

This 1899 view of Church Street looking east, shows the Cutlers' Hall (p47) with its 1888 extended frontage, and the Sheffield & Hallamshire Bank (p44).

Beyond the Cutler's Hall stands the Cole Brothers Building (p54) on the corner of Fargate.

[1899 p77]

The view of Fargate, with 'Cole's Corner' on the right is also a result of the 1890's redevelopment of the city centre. Though many of the buildings have since been replaced, several roof lines can still be recognized, most notably the Town Hall, which was opened in 1897 by Queen Victoria.

[1899 p110]

VIEW OF FARGATE.

MESSRS. COCKAYNE'S NEW PREMISES, ANGEL STREET.

The Cockayne brothers, Thomas Bagshawe and William, opened a draper's shop on Angel Street in 1829. The company bought up neighbouring property to extend the site and in 1898 they built the new premises shown here.

Innovations in the 1898 store included an arcade (shown right) which replaced the previous alleyway of Watson Walk. The walk was widened to 12 ft. (3.6 m.), covered by a 95 ft. (29 m.) long glass roof, and paved with marble mosaic.

The store was destroyed in the Blitz of 1940, and was rebuilt between 1949 and 1955. In this redevelopment the path of the arcade was retained as a through way from Angel Street to Hartshead which still preserves the name of Watson Walk (now Watson's Walk).

In 1972 Cockayne's were taken over by Schofield's and the store finally closed in 1982.

[1899 p113] & [1899 p113]

MESSRS. COCKAYNE'S NEW ARCADE.

- 53 -

MESSRS. COLE BROTHERS, CHURCH-STREET AND FARGATE.

John, Thomas and Skelton Cole opened their business as Silk Mercers and Hatters in 1847 at 4, Fargate. The building shown here was completed in 1869 at the corner of Fargate and Church Street, creating the famous 'Cole's Corner'.

In 1919 the business was sold to the Selfridge empire but continued to operate as Cole Brothers, and in 1940 the 'Selfridge Provincial Stores Group' was sold to the John Lewis Partnership.

The building came through the Sheffield Blitz, and survived until the business moved in 1963 to more spacious premises in Barker's Pool. The new store was built on the site of the old Albert Hall which had been demolished after a fire in 1937.

The 1869 building was demolished and Cole's Corner was redeveloped in 1964.

The Cole Brothers name was changed to John Lewis in 2002.

[1879 p145]

Industry

BESSEMER STEEL SHOP—MESSRS. BESSEMER AND CO. LIMITED.

IRON AND STEEL—CRUDE AND MANUFACTURED.

A large part of each of the Guides dealt with Sheffield's various industries, a major proportion being related to iron and steel.

The illustrations which follow here are loosely arranged to bring together views of the related works at different times. 'Loosely' because most of the manufacturers were involved in many aspects of the industry – from raw iron to specialist steels, and from cannon to crinolines.

[1879 p200]

Metal working in Sheffield was originally based on a combination of local ironstone, plentiful wood and later coal, and the motive power supplied by the fast flowing upland streams.

By 1557 Danish and Swedish iron was being imported, and provided the ideal raw material for the evolution of a vast range of techniques and products which, over the next 300 years, made Sheffield a world-leading centre for processing iron and steel.

This casting was made from crucible steel by Hadfield's Steel Foundry for the 1878 Paris Exhibition to demonstrate the quality of work which was central to Sheffield's success.

[1879 p241]

Wortley Top Forge is one of the oldest surviving works in the area, and dates from the 17th century. The date stone shown here relates to alterations made in 1713 and is still on display at the Top Forge.

The forge was located to take advantage of the water power available from the River Don, and was typical of the small works which developed along every tributary of the river.

[1879 p320, 1889 p125, 1899 p194]

As the industry expanded, the small works tied to fast flowing streams were replaced by larger integrated works needing more power. Steam power needed access to coal, and the industry moved further down the Don valley toward the canal and along the growing rail network.

The simple hammer shown on the Wortley date stone was the forerunner of the tilt hammers seen in this 1862 illustration at Sanderson Brothers in Attercliffe.

[1862 p117, 1879 p211]

STEEL TILTING. - MESSRS SANDERSON BROTHERS AND CO, ATTERCLIFFE.

B. HUNTSMAN, STEEL FURNACES & OFFICES, ATTERCLIFFE.

Prior to 1740, steel was made by heating bar-iron with charcoal in conical 'cementation' furnaces – as seen in the centre of this illustration. The iron did not melt and the resulting 'blister steel' was inconsistent. Benjamin Huntsman, a Doncaster clockmaker then living in Handsworth, developed a method of melting the blister steel in a 'crucible' furnace – easily recognised by their stack of flues seen on the right of the view. This produced 'cast' or 'refined' steel, the quality of which was ideal for specialist applications.

[1889 p133]

Huntsman also operated the Wicker Tilt to the NE of Lady's Bridge – the bridge is seen on the left of this illustration. The weir provided the power for the tilt mill, and can still be seen under the bridge.

The building carries the date 1751. It operated until 1900, when it was demolished and the site used for the Royal Exchange Building, built for John Henry Bryars, an animal breeder and vet. The adjacent building, Castle House, was a multi-storey stables, later converted into a pea-canning factory for Batchelors, and then a furniture store for Hancock and Lant.

[1889 p133]

B. HUNTSMAN, WICKER FORGE, LADY'S BRIDGE.

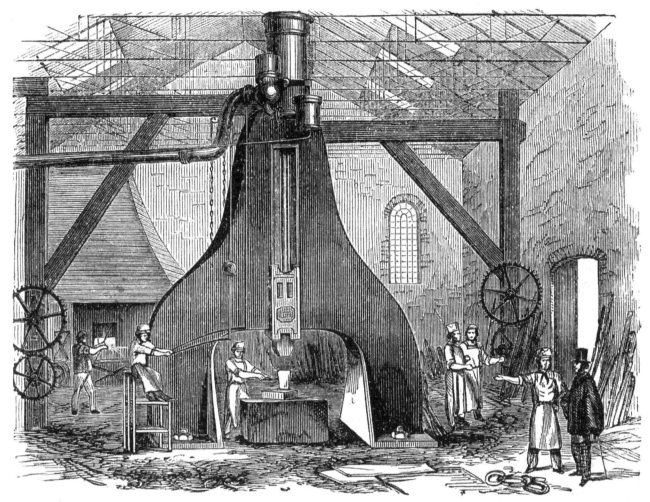

STEAM HAMMER.—MESSRS. SANDERSON BROTHERS AND CO., ATTERCLIFFE.

In the 1840s, James Nasmyth, a Scottish engineer, devised a steam powered hammer which was more versatile than the tilt-hammers then in use. Though the first working machine was made in France by François Bourdon, very soon they were in use in many works in Sheffield.

The steam hammer reduced costs by as much as 50% and as well as increasing quality also allowed the forging of larger pieces. It was one of the many developments which drove the growth of the industry through the 19th century. For some purposes tilt hammers were still used, but by 1879 the steam hammer was used for most forgings. For many uses, they have now been superseded by hydraulic and mechanical presses.

[1862 p118, 1879 p213]

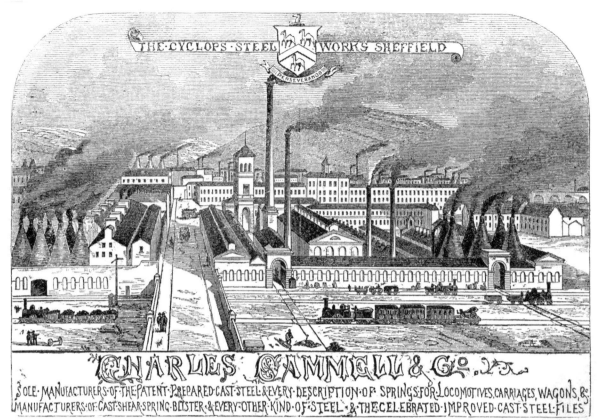

CYCLOPS STEEL IRON, AND SPRING WORKS.—MESSRS. C. CAMMELL AND CO.

In 1842 Cyclops Works were the first works to be built beside the Sheffield & Rotherham Railway after the railay opened in 1838.

Johnson, Cammell and Co. were established in 1837 in Furnival Street. In 1855 they became Charles Cammell and Co., and over the next century went through many name changes becoming Cammell Laird in 1903. Their steel making arm became part of the English Steel Corporation in 1928 and British Steel in 1967.

Cyclops Works stood beside Sutherland Street, seen above in the 1862 view facing SE towards Saville Street. The line of the railway from Wicker station still exists as President Way, a road running between industrial units.

The 1899 view (right) shows the growth of the works. Saville Street is in the foreground, and a large part of the works are now beyond the railway towards Carlisle Street.

[1862 p125] & [1899 p178]

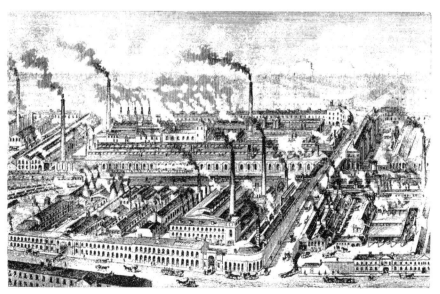

CYCLOPS WORKS—MESSRS CHARLES CAMMELL AND COMPANY LIMITED.

The pair of conical cementation furnaces in the distance were part of the integrated nature of Cyclops works, providing blister steel which would be 'refined' in the crucible furnaces.

The forge shop, with its individual hearths and distinctive row of chimneys, was another common feature of such a works.

[1862 p127]

FORGE SHOP.—MESSRS. C. CAMMELL AND CO., CYCLOPS WORKS.

The view below, also within Cyclops Works, shows the process of making crucible steel. New crucibles can be seen drying on the shelves on the left, while below are the furnace holes in which the crucibles are heated.

The baskets on the left will contain measured amounts of the raw materials, ready for 'charging' the crucibles.

The man on the left is testing a crucible to decide whether the steel is ready for pouring.

Two men in the centre are pouring the content of a crucible into an ingot mould.

[1862 p113, 1879 p207]

STEEL CASTING SHOP—MESSRS. C. CAMMELL AND CO.. CYCLOPS WORKS.

STEEL ROLLING MILLS.—MESSRS. C. CAMMELL AND CO., CYCLOPS WORKS.

The series of rollers running down the centre of the building are driven by the steam engine on the right.

Ingots would be reheated in furnaces shown on the left of the illustration, before being passed back and forth through the rollers decreasing the size in stages as required.

[1862 p115]

Railway springs were just one of the products made at Cyclops Works. Steel strips would be cut to length and shaped according to their ultimate purpose. The leaves would then be riveted together to form the completed spring.

The 1862 Guide was keen to explain these processes, and the way in which Cammells tested each completed spring as well as the metal itself.

[1862 p129]

SPRING SHOP.—MESSRS. C. CAMMELL AND CO, CYCLOPS WORKS.

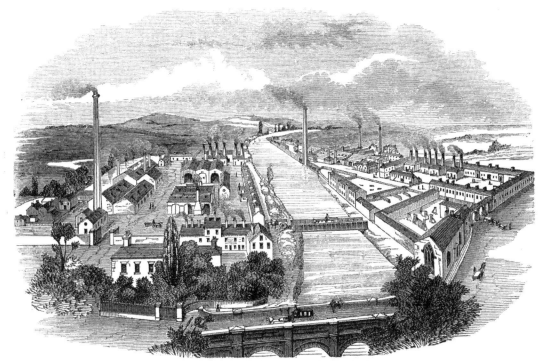

BRIGHTSIDE STEEL WORKS.—MESSRS W. JESSOP AND SONS.

The Jessops were an old Sheffield family, and one of the few firms in Sheffield exclusively involved in steel making. In the early 19th century they had works in Furnival Street in the town centre, and in Blast Lane near the canal basin (p64). Starting out as Mitchell, Raikes and Jessop in 1774, in 1832 the company took the name William Jessop and Sons, and in 1835 they built their new works in the open countryside of Brightside.

By 1879 the Brightside Works covered over thirty acres and had three miles of internal railways, including a direct link into the Midland line (formerly the Sheffield and Rotherham).

The works closed in the late 1980s. Only the former gateway of the works remains as a monument within an office park, known as 'Jessop's Riverside'. Much of the site remains undeveloped.

[1862 p120] & [1879 p217, 1889 p131]

WILLIAM JESSOP & SONS, LIMITED. BRIGHTSIDE STEEL WORKS, SHEFFIELD.

This illustration from the 1862 Guide shows two other works operated by Jessops.

Park Steel Works stood at the junction of Blast Lane and Navigation Hill. It was built in about 1830, and so predates the move to Brightside.

The tramway in the foreground ran from Manor Pit down to the canal and on to the Manor Coal Yard by the Canal Basin.

The works were demolished in 1898 to make way for a railway goods yard, and the site is now covered by the Parkway.

Soho Mills were a later addition which stood in the town centre on Pond Street at the bottom of Baker's Hill. It produced sheet steel, especially for pen making, largely for Birmingham pen makers.

[1862 p121]

SOHO STEEL ROLLING MILLS.—MESSRS. W. JESSOP AND SONS.

STEEL BELL CASTING—RIVER DON WORKS.

Naylor, Vickers & Co. were the first company in Britain to cast finished objects in steel rather than casting ingots for further processing. In 1854 they acquired a German patent to cast steel bells, and in 1862 a bell weighing 4½ tons was produced. This required 176 crucibles to be poured as a continuous stream to ensure there were no flaws in the casting. The process took just 11 minutes. At the time it was the largest steel casting ever made in Britain.

Steel bells had advantages over those made in bell metal, a form of bronze. They were cheaper to make and were lighter, and they could still be rung safely in freezing temperatures in which a bronze bell would crack. Unfortunately they made an inferior sound and were not popular. Vickers made their last steel bells in 1885.

A peal of bells made by Naylor, Vickers & Co. were installed in St. Marie's Roman Catholic Church in Sheffield (p20) in 1862, but were moved to St. Mary's, Moseley, Birmingham, in 1874. They were rung for the last time in January 2012 and have now been replaced by 'traditional' bells.

A set of Naylor Vickers bells made in 1856 hang in the Millennium Gallery in Sheffield.

By 1870 the same process was used to cast a steel marine drive shaft weighing 22 tons and requiring 672 crucibles, and by 1879 castings were made weighing up to 30 tons. By 1899, the Guide describes castings of 70 to 100 tons but the steel was most likely made by the Siemens Open-Hearth process.

[1862 p123, 1879 p219, 1889 p135]

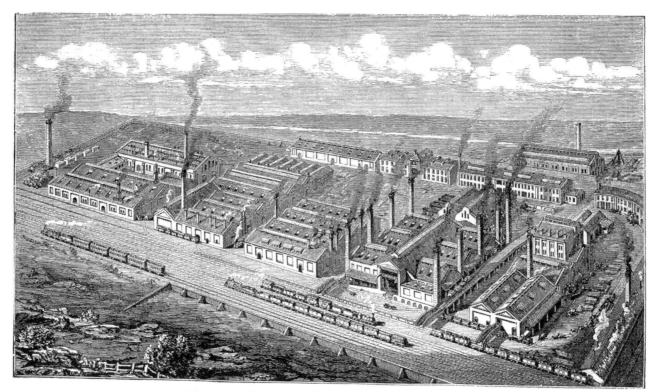

RIVER DON WORKS——MESSRS. VICKERS, SONS AND CO. LIMITED.

The firm of Naylor, Vickers and Co. was first formed in 1829, and had works at Millsands near Lady's Bridge, and at Wadsley. It was at the Millsands Works that they produced their steel bells (p65) - the works even had its own bell tower in order to test the bells it made.

In 1862 the company began to build their new River Don Works alongside the Midland Railway near Brightside. The new works, seen above in 1879, lacked conical cementation furnaces, suggesting that the crucible furnaces were using a process patented by Thomas Vickers to directly use a mixture of Swedish bar-iron and cast-iron. The cast iron provided the carbon which would otherwise have been added in the cementation process.

Vickers became a major producer of naval guns and armour plate, and in 1897 acquired the Maxim-Nordenfeldt Gun and Ammunition Co. to become Vickers, Sons and Maxim. Through the 20th century, the company had interests in fields as diverse as ship building, car production, aircraft manufacture, bottling plants and scientific instruments.

The works, now operated by Sheffield Forgemasters, still straddle Brightside Lane. Parts of the buildings are now Grade II listed.

[1879 p218, 1889 p134]

BESSEMER STEEL SHOP—MESSRS. BESSEMER AND CO. LIMITED.

The use of cementation and crucible processes, as seen at Cyclops Works (p61), required high-quality low-carbon wrought iron which was largely imported from Sweden. The cementation process would add the carbon necessary to form steel, and the crucible furnace would ensure an even consistent quality in the cast metal.

In 1856, Henry Bessemer (1813-1858) announced a new process for making steel in bulk. Bessemer's process could take lower quality pig iron direct from a blast furnace. This had a high carbon content, and by blowing air through the molten metal would reduce the carbon to the required level for making steel. At the same time other impurities would be burnt off. The result was not as a high a quality as crucible steel, but was ideal for bulk manufacturing of products such as steel rails for the expanding railways.

While a crucible processed up to 60 lbs. (27 kg.) of blister steel, the Bessemer Converter used raw iron, could hold 30 tons, and the process was reduced from several hours to under half an hour.

Bessemer set up his own works in Carlisle Street in 1858, in part to persuade other producers to adopt his process. Very soon other works such as Cyclops and Atlas Works were all making Bessemer steel under licence.

In the above illustration a pair of 'converters' are operating in tandem, the one on the left is being 'blown', while on the right the finished steel is being poured into a ladle for transfer into the ingot moulds shown in the foreground.

[1879 p231, 1889 p147, 1899 p218]

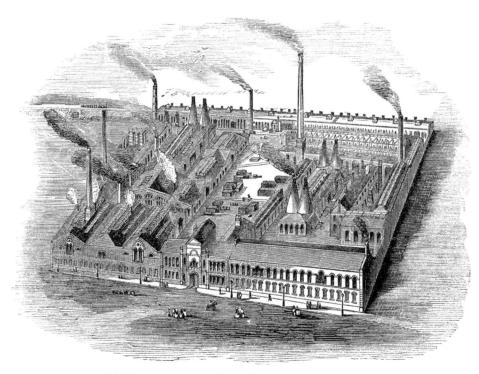

ATLAS STEEL, IRON, AND SPRING WORKS — MESSRS. JOHN BROWN AND CO.

The first Atlas Works had been built in the 1840s in Furnival Street. In 1857 John Brown moved his company, and the name, to a new greenfield site lying between the Midland Railway and what became Saville Street East, close to Cammell's Cyclops Works. This 1862 illustration omitted recent extensions seen below in the 1879 view.

[1862 p132]

The original works (seen in the foreground below) extended within three years from 3 acres to 30 acres, and by 1859 Brown was producing rails for the quickly expanding railway industry using the new Bessemer process.

Brown died in 1896 and in 1902 the company began working with Thomas Firth and Sons, finally merging in 1930 to form Firth Brown. The Atlas site was cleared in the 1980s and is now occupied by industrial units.

[1879 p233, 1889 p151]

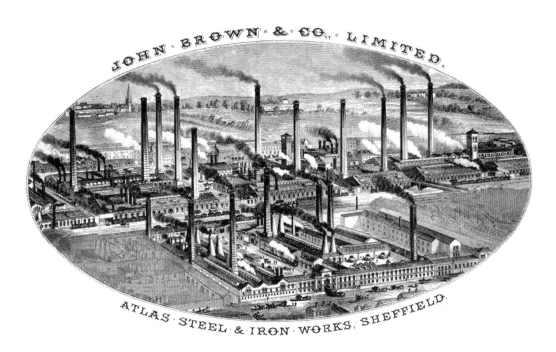

JOHN BROWN & CO. LIMITED.

ATLAS STEEL & IRON WORKS, SHEFFIELD.

ARMOUR PLATE ROLLING.

Armour plate was originally made from slabs of red-hot 'puddled iron' which were hammered together to form a laminated plate. The process would be repeated until several hundred such slabs had been converted into a single plate, providing the structure which gave the strength in the finished plate.

The rolling of armour plate was pioneered by John Brown and Co. and this greatly increased the potential size and thickness of the finished plates. In the illustration above at Brown's Atlas Works, a red-hot piece is being dragged from the furnace to the rolling mill on the right. As more layers were added, the piece would need to be returned to the furnace to be heated ready for the next stage of rolling. By 1862, these plates could already weigh as much as 11 tons.

A facing layer of steel was added to the iron armour in a patent taken out in 1876, and by 1899 all-steel armour was being used exclusively. This was produced using bulk steel produced largely by the Siemens Open-Hearth process which was developed in the 1860s – like the Bessemer converter, this process removed excess carbon from the raw pig iron, but proved to be easier to control, allowed more flexibility by allowing the use of scrap iron and steel, and provided greater production capacity. In 1899, John Brown & Co. were producing 10,000 tons of armour plate per year.

The advances in armour plate were being made by the same companies that were also producing ever larger and more powerful guns and ordnance, often in the same works.

[1862 p131, 1879 p235, 1889 p153]

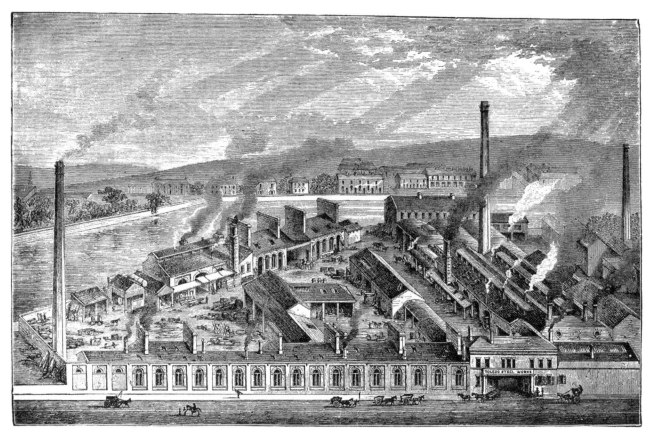

TOLEDO STEEL WORKS—MESSRS J. H. ANDREW AND CO.

John Henry Andrew established his first steel works in 1856, and operated from Malinda Street, near Shalesmoor, from 1860 to 1870 when he erected the Toledo Works between Neepsend Lane and the River Don. He died in 1884 and the works were continued by his sons. In the 20th century they became Andrews Toledo.

[1879 p228, 1889 p145] & [1899 p207]

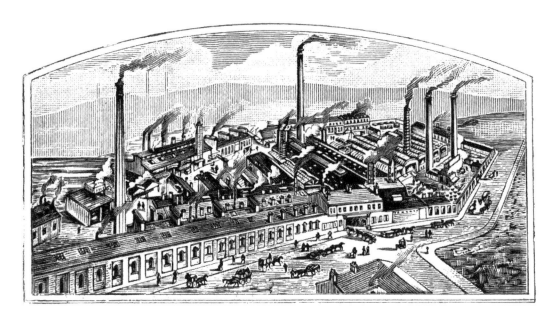

TOLEDO WORKS.

J. H. Andrew & Co. made a wide variety of products. These ranged from rifle barrels, swords and bayonets, to mining tools, and springs for a range of vehicles. One speciality was wire rolling. For the Paris Exhibition in 1878 they rolled a 270 lb. (122 kg.) ingot into an unbroken 'rod' almost half a mile long (685 m.). It was said that most of the cables in American suspension bridges were made at Toledo Works.

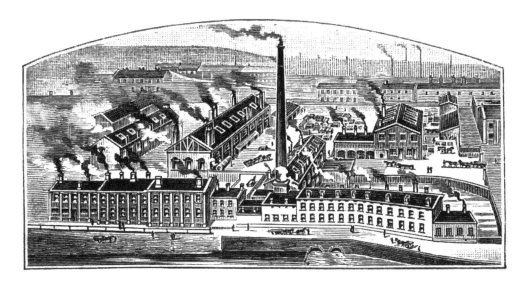

CLIFTON WORKS.

The Andrews company also owned two other works shown in the 1899 Guide. Clifton Works also stood by the river in Neepsend, immediately north of Hillfoot Bridge and the Farfield Inn. Effingham Road Works were to the east of the town, towards Attercliffe.

[1899 p207]

EFFINGHAM ROAD WORKS.

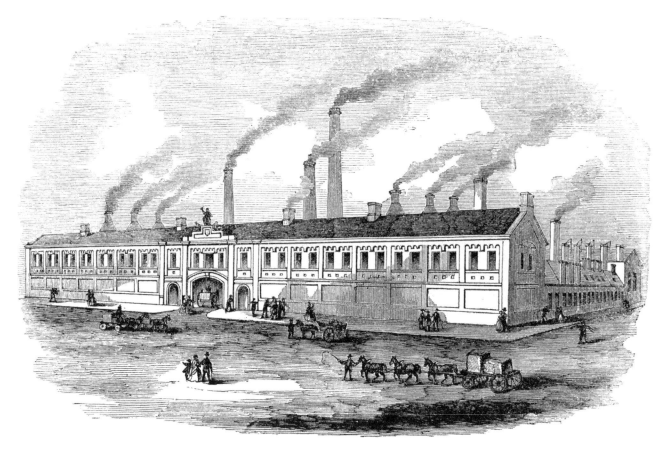

REGENT WORKS.—MESSRS. BURYS AND CO., MANUFACTURERS OF STEEL, FILES, SAWS, EDGE TOOLS, ETC.

Edward Bury (1794-1858) was born in Salford, Lancashire. After a career as a locomotive maker and after three years in partnership with Charles Cammell, in 1855 he joined the partnership of Bedford, Burys & Co., at Regent Works, on the junction of Penistone Road and Rutland Road, now the site of a Wickes retail store.

The lower 1879 view of Regent Works includes Bury's Philadelphia Rolling Mills and Forge, standing on the opposite side of Rutland Road – the Rutland Road bridge over the Don can be seen in distance.

[1862 p133] & [1879 p221, 1889 p137, 1899 p215]

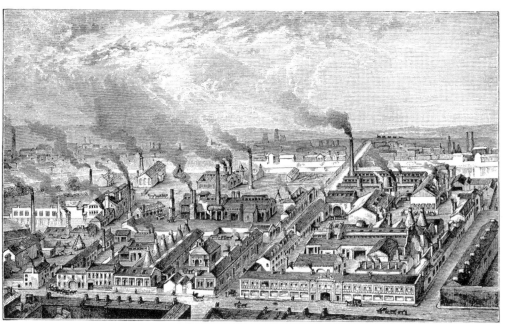

REGENT WORKS—MESSRS. BURYS AND CO. LIMITED.

CLYDE STEEL AND IRON WORKS—MESSRS. SAMUEL OSBORN AND CO.

The inset of this 1879 illustration shows the original Clyde Works set up by Samuel Osborn in Broad Lane in 1851, later renamed Brookhill Works.

The new Clyde Works, lying between the Wicker and the River Don, were bought by Osborn in 1868.

Among a wide range of products, Osborn had sole rights to produce special steels developed by Robert Mushet, an iron master from the Forest of Dean. These included a range of self-hardening and tool steels.

The foreground of this view of the works shows the offices built in the Wicker in 1853 for Shortridge and Howell, the previous owners of the works. These are now occupied by the SADACCA Community Centre.

[1879 p226]

This 1889 view of Clyde Works is from the east with Blonk Street bridge in the foreground. The turreted Castle or Tower Grinding Wheel can be seen by the river – this was demolished along with the rest of the works in about 1970.

[1889 p139]

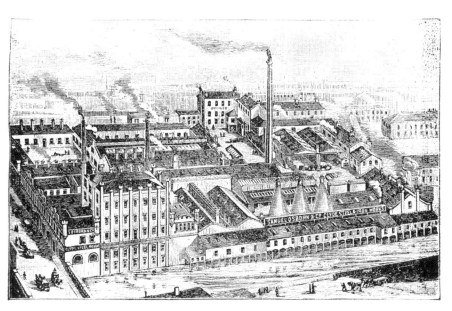

CLYDE STEEL AND IRON WORKS.

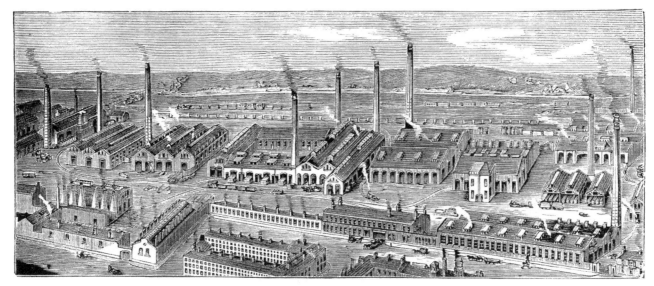

SHEFFIELD STEEL AND IRON WORKS——MESSRS. BROWN, BAYLEY AND DIXON LIMITED.

Brown, Bayley and Dixon Limited were established in 1873 by George Brown, nephew of John Brown of the Atlas Works. Their works were built in Attercliffe alongside the Manchester, Sheffield & Lincolnshire Railway and the Sheffield Canal. In 1990 the former works became the site of the Don Valley Stadium, now itself closed.

The company, later Brown Bayley Steels, specialised in steel rails and tyres. The works were designed to take in raw materials such as pig iron directly from the railway, and also for the finished products to be transported by rail to the customer.

[1879 p237, 1889 p156, 1899 p212]

Sheffield's steel industry depended on a supply of high quality iron, made from low phosphorus ores such as those mined in the Dannemora region of Sweden. Dannemora gave its name to the works of Seebohm and Dieckstahl, acquired in 1869, which stood behind the Wicker beside the River Don, next to Osborn's Clyde Works.

Though Henry Seebohm was born in Bradford, by 1915 anti-German feelings prompted the company to change its name to Arthur Balfour and Co. Balfour was then the MD of the company, and in 1911 had been Master Cutler.

[1899 p210]

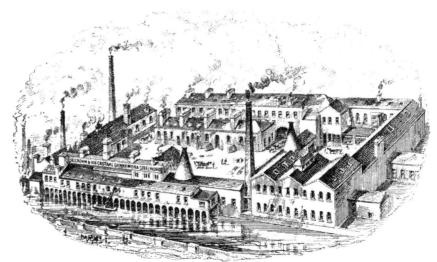

DANNEMORA STEEL WORKS.——MESSRS SEEBOHM AND DIECKSTAHL.

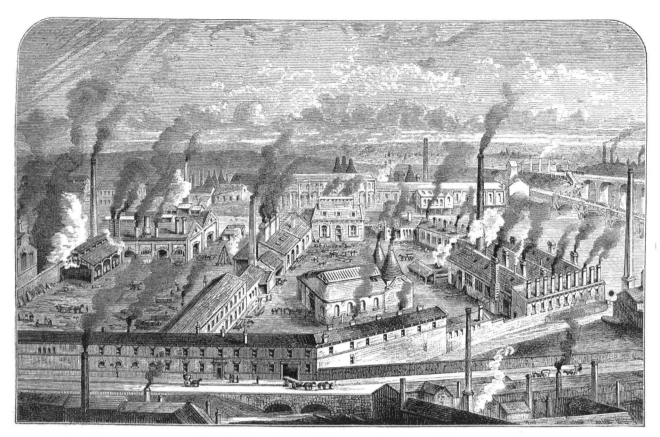

SCOTIA STEEL WORKS—MESSRS. THOMAS JOWITT AND SONS.

In 1848 Thomas Jowitt started his steel making business at Saville Works in Saville Street. He later moved to Royds Works on Warren Street, and then in 1864 erected Scotia Steel Works. The new works stood across Warren Street from Royds Works,

The view here, facing SW, has Warren Street in the foreground crossing the mill race. The River Don is to the right (west) and beyond it can be seen Norfolk Bridge and the viaduct which still carries the railway running from Midland Station towards Meadowhall. By the viaduct are the covered steps leading up to the former Attercliffe Road Station.

Scotia Steel Works were renamed Crescent Steel Works in 1901, and in the mid 20th century were operated by Walter Spencer and Co. Ltd.

Little now remains of the works, except possibly part of the frontage seen in the lower left of the illustration.

[1879 p223, 1889 p138]

JONAS AND COLVER,

Joseph Jonas came to Sheffield from Germany and started his steel making business in 1874, where he was joined by Robert Colver, of Pilot Works on Cotton Mill Row, off Corporation Street. Originally producing crucible steel, by 1899 they were producing a wide range of special steels.

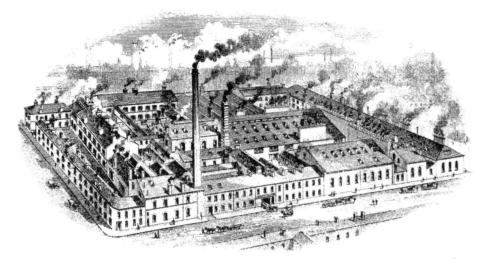

CONTINENTAL STEEL WORKS,
SHEFFIELD.

Continental Works stood on Bessemer Road, Attercliffe. In 1899 they also operated the Universal Steel Works shown below.

[1889 p143]

William Thomas Beesley was a director of the limited company formed by Jonas and Colver in 1892, and it is said in the 1899 Guide that Beesley's Universal Works were also run by the new company.

Universal Steel Works stood between Attercliffe Road (in foreground) and Effingham Street (in the distance on left) and spanned the River Don with its own linking bridge. Attercliffe Road Station is on the left.

[1889 p143]

W. T. BEESLEY & CO. LIMITED,

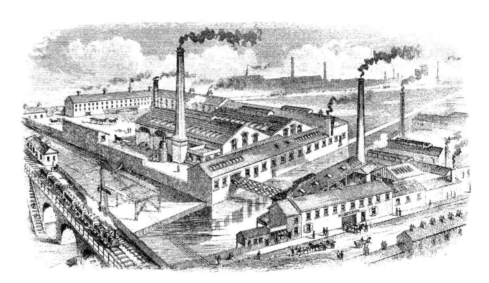

UNIVERSAL STEEL, WIRE, HOT AND COLD ROLLING MILLS,
SHEFFIELD.

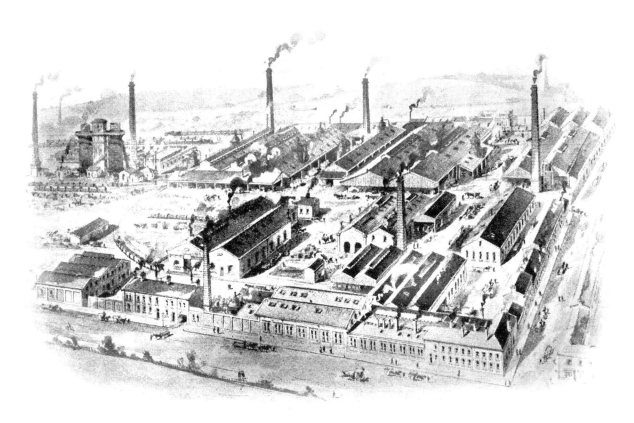

VIEW OF WORKS.—MESSRS. WILLIAM COOKE AND COMPANY LIMITED.

William Cooke's Tinsley Steel, Iron, and Wire Rope Works were established in 1866 on a green-field site on Attercliffe Common beside the Manchester, Sheffield & Lincolnshire Railway (later the Great Central Railway and now the route of the Supertram).

The integration within the works included the production of their own pig-iron – the blast furnace can be seen in the distance on the left of illustration.

The 1899 Guide describes their operations in some detail, wire being just one of their many products. A 'more modern branch of their trade' is also described – the manufacture of horse shoes, said to be 'developing rapidly'.

In the 20th century, Cooke's were acquired by British Ropes and later operated as Tinsley Wire Industries finally becoming part of the Belgian company Betafence. The works were closed In 2006, and in May 2013 a planning application was submitted to build an IKEA store on the site. The application has recently been approved by the city council.

[1899 p231]

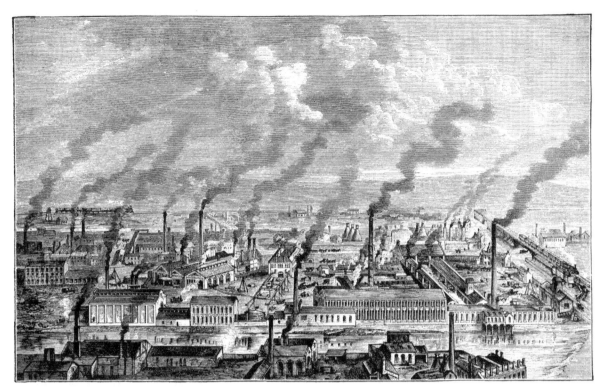

PARK IRON WORKS—MESSRS. DAVY BROTHERS LIMITED.

All of the works in Sheffield relied on engineering companies and boiler makers, one of the largest being Davy Brothers. They were established in 1830 at the Soho Foundry and Engine Works, Pear Street, now under Corporation Street. In 1840 Davy's built the first railway locomotive in Sheffield, for the Sheffield & Rotherham Railway. They moved to Park Iron Works, between Foley Street and the river in about 1850. These were demolished in 2007.

Scotia Steel Works (p75) can be seen in the foreground, Attercliffe Road Station on the right, and the Manchester, Sheffield & Lincolnshire Railway (later the Great Central Railway) in the background.

[1879 p291]

The Don Tool Works in Mowbray Street, across the River Don from Kelham Island, were leased in 1858 by Robert Francis Drury, Ensor Drury and Joel Eaton Walker. They were damaged in the Great Sheffield Flood in 1864, and the company's premises and machinery were sold by auction in 1870.

[1862 p162]

INTERIOR OF MESSRS. DRURY BROTHERS AND WALKER'S FITTING AND ERECTING SHOP.

WORKS OF MESSRS. COCKER BROTHERS, MANUFACTURERS OF STEEL WIRE, FILES, ETC.

The use of cast crucible steel provided a consistent product which was ideal for the production of wire. Cocker Brothers were pioneers in this trade. Established in 1752, their wire mills were in Nursery Street, close to Lady's Bridge.

They also made steel at Wardsend (now Rawson Spring Road), and Navigation Steel Works (probably on Blast Lane, near the Canal Basin), also shown in the illustration.

The 1862 Guide gives an eloquent description of the processes involved, and the range of products for which the wire was used. The wire used in watch motions was said to be worth as much as gold, one pound (450 gm.) of steel would make a wire 552,960 inches long (14 km.).

[1862 p164]

John Hartley's Newhall Wire Mills were located in what had been open fields by the River Don. In 1850 this was the site of a smaller works, close to New Hall, then as isolated country house. In 1836, the area was described as 'a pleasant walk along the river side – not yet quite obliterated'.

The works were shown in 1890 as Newhall Iron Works. The site is now Riverside Court business units.

[1879 p246]

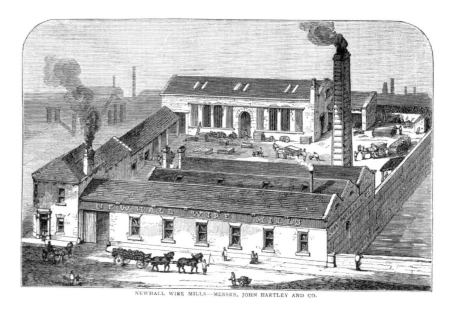

NEWHALL WIRE MILLS—MESSRS. JOHN HARTLEY AND CO.

SAW GRINDING.

In the early days of the metal working industry in Sheffield, each trade would work in isolation on the different processes that went to make a finished article. Many of the small works which grew up on the fast flowing streams were used by grinders, and each would specialise in one specific type of product, such as knives, scissors, files, scythes, etc.

Saw grinding as seen here was one such speciality.

[1879 p279, 1889 p176]

By the middle of the 19th century, the works were becoming more centralised and more integrated. Power was now provided by steam engines, and the isolated grinders were brought together in larger workshops. These workshops would also be located within a works which might bring together all of the processes to take raw materials and produce a finished article, ready for sale. Some of the works even included their own show-rooms from which the products were sold.

[1862 p136, 1879 p250]

A SHEFFIELD GRINDERS' "HULL."

MESSRS. BEARDSHAW AND SONS, MANUFACTURERS OF STEEL, FILES, SAWS, ETC.

The firm of John Beardshaw and Sons was founded in 1719 and from 1726 operated from Hollis Croft, and later from Garden Street. They continued to produce tools under their 'Conqueror', 'Invincible' and 'Vigilant' labels through the 20th century.

Beardshaw's Baltic Works were built in 1854, and stand between Effingham Road and the canal, east of Bacon Lane. Now Grade II listed, they have been converted to industrial units.

The opening scenes of 'The Full Monty' were filmed on the canal behind the Baltic Works.

[1862 p149]

Jonathan Beet, Sons and Griffith, established on Broad Lane in 1845, built Agenoria Works in 1852 on Saville Street East (NE of Sutherland Street). Agenoria Works were one of the succession of new works built beside the new railway to Rotherham.

The works were later run by Peace, Ward and Co. and after this partnership was dissolved in 1867 they became part of Charles Cammell's Cyclops Works.

[1862 p148]

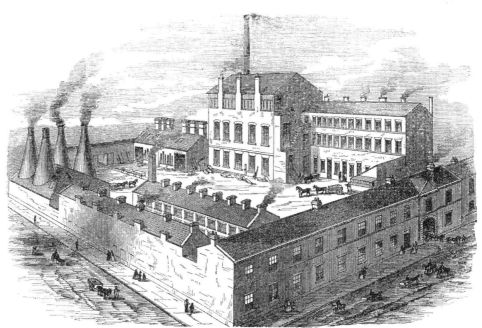

AGENORIA WORKS.—MESSRS. PEACE, WARD, AND CO., MANUFACTURERS OF STEEL, FILES, EDGE TOOLS, ETC.

ALMA WORKS.—MR. WILLIAM HALL, MANUFACTURER OF STEEL, FILES, SAWS, ETC.

As the new factories expanded along the Don valley some works remained within the town centre. The 1862 Guide gives this illustration of William Hall's Alma Works which stood between Orchard Lane and Barker's Pool – now the site of the Fountain Precinct.

The 1862 guide notes the emphasis within the buildings on improving the working conditions in such matters as providing adequate ventilation.

The works continued with various occupants, including Spear and Jackson, into the 20th century and were replaced (? in 1910) by the Grand Hotel which closed in 1971.

[1862 p159, 1879 p264, 1889 p171]

Until the 1860s file cutting was done by hand. The smooth piece of steel was 'cut' using a sharp chisel struck up to 100 times per minute by a hammer which could weigh up to 6 lb. (2.7 kg.).

Sheffield workmen argued that files made by machines, invented in the 1860s, were inferior to hand made. This led to a sixteen week strike in 1866.

Files continued to be made by hand, as well as by machine, into the 20th century.

[1862 p147, 1879 p261, 1889 p169]

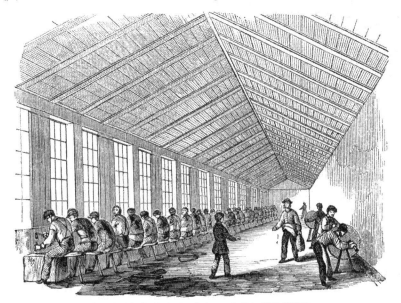

FILE CUTTERS' SHOP.—W. HALL AND SON, ALMA WORKS.

SHEAF WORKS—MESSRS. THOMAS TURTON AND SONS.

William Greaves was listed as a cutler in Burgess Street in 1787. By 1817 he had moved to Division Street, and in the 1820s, together with his sons Edward and Richard, built Sheaf Works as the first integrated steel works in Sheffield. The works straddled the canal, which had opened in 1819, the parts being linked by the Cadman Street Bridge seen on the right. They pre-dated the building of the railway, which crossed the site, and the Victoria Station seen here in the distance.

The works were transferred to Eyre, Wood and Co. in 1855 and Thomas Turton and Sons in 1858. The Thomas Turton company was bought by Frederick Thorpe Mappin in 1860 and continued as a steel producer in Sheffield until 1980. The name is still used by their new owners, Padley & Venables Ltd., based in Dronfield.

The works offices on the left are still standing and are now Grade II listed. They are now called Sheaf Quay. When refurbished in 1996 they briefly became a pub, but by 2001 they had been converted to offices.

[1862 p151, 1879 p224]

ETNA WORKS.—MESSRS. SPEAR AND JACKSON.

The origins of the firm of Spear and Jackson can be traced back to 1760 when Alexander Spear joined John Love in his business making saws from crucible steel. Spear's nephew John later ran the company and in 1820 was joined by Samuel Jackson. Their partnership was set up in 1830.

Etna (or Ætna) Works were among the works built on Saville Street East in 1852, backing onto the Midland Railway, and just beyond Cyclops Works and Sutherland Street. Cammell's Bridge can be seen in the background on the left.

The Spear and Jackson Group is now part of Neill Tools, and their HQ is still in Sheffield, less than half a mile from their old Etna Works.

[1862 p155, 1879 p280]

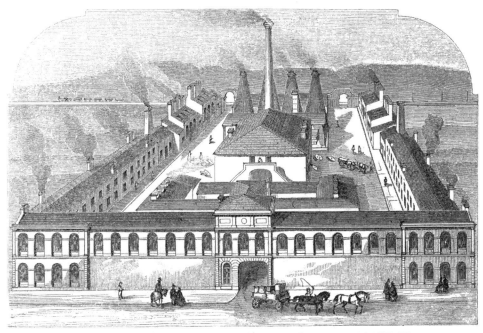

PRESIDENT WORKS.—MESSRS. MOSES EADON AND SONS, MANUFACTURERS OF SAWS, FILES, STEEL, ETC.

Moses Eadon established his company in 1823 in Norfolk Street, in the centre of the town, and transferred to Saville Street East in 1852. President Works were another of the works built in that year (e.g. p84) on green-field sites between Saville Street East and the Midland Railway (seen in the background).

The firm specialised in saw making, and in 1856 took out a patent for a continuous band saw.

By 1857 President Works were surrounded by John Brown's Atlas Works and Thomas Firth's Norfolk Works.

The company continued into the 20th century, and in 1918 Moses Eadon and Sons were absorbed into Sheffield Steel Products, based at Templeborough. The works became part of the Atlas Works.

The frontage of the works, including the gateway seen in these illustrations, still stands on Saville Street East and is Grade II listed.

[1862 p157] & [1899 p227]

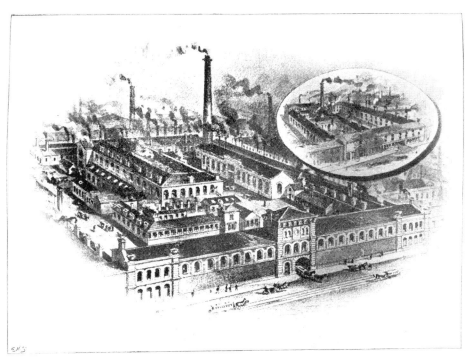

PRESIDENT WORKS—MESSRS. MOSES EADON AND SONS.

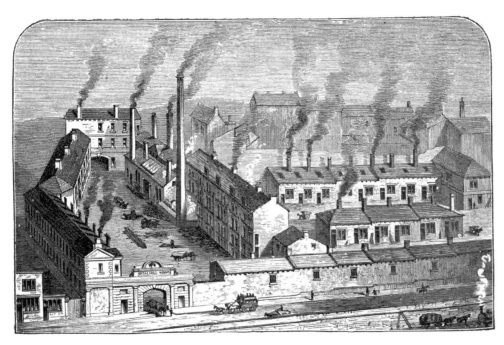

MESSRS. JOHN SORBY AND SONS—SPITAL-HILL WORKS.

John Sorby, Master Cutler in 1806 and a descendant of the first Master Cutler in 1624, worked with his sons, John and Henry on the Wicker in 1797. They built Spital Hill Works in 1823.

By 1849 the company had been acquired by Lockwood Brothers, cousins of the Sorby family, who retained the trade-marks 'I. and H. Sorby' and 'Pampa'.

[1879 p274]

John Sorby and Sons were the first Sheffield makers of sheep shears – the 1879 Guide includes the illustration on the right and a detailed description of their manufacture.

Parts of the same family, possibly the same John, were also involved in a short lived venture 'Sorby and Turner' with the trade-mark 'I. Sorby', later used by Joseph Turner and Co.

Other branches of the family were also involved in the tool trade. Robert Sorby & Sons, started by John's nephew in 1828, still produce tools in Sheffield.

[1879 p275]

SHEAR BENDING AND FINISHING ROOM.

MESSRS. LOCKWOOD BROTHERS, ARUNDEL-STREET

Lockwood Brothers also operated from Sterling Works in Arundel Street (N of Froggatt Lane). The building is now Grade II listed and is part of Freeman College.

In 1919 Lockwood's and several other firms including Joseph Elliot and Sons were merged as Sheffield Cutlery Manufacturers Ltd.

In 1923 Joseph Elliot and Sons moved to the Sorby's former Spital Hill Works, and in 1926 the company was sold back to Joseph Greaves Elliot who moved production to Granville Works on Sylvester Street. They continued to use Sorby's 'Pampa' trade-mark through the 20th century.

[1879 p274]

The illustrations on the right are views of Lockwood's Arundel Street Works. The first shows a typical crucible steel melting shop not unlike that shown on p61.

The Cutlers Shop brings together various processes involved in finishing cutlery, such as hafting and polishing.

The illustration of file forging shows the type of machines which took over from the hand file forging seen on p82.

[1879 p275]

STEEL MELTING FURNACE.

CUTLERS' SHOP.

FILE FORGING SHOP.

HIBERNIA WORKS—MESSRS. WILLIAM MARPLES AND SONS.

In 1821 the 12 year old William Marples Junior joined his father's joinery business in Sheffield. In 1828 at the age of 19, he was trading under his own name as a tool maker in Broomhall Street, moving in 1837 to Broomspring Lane. In 1856 the company moved to Hibernia Works in Westfield Terrace above Division Street, and the company remained there until 1972 when production moved to Dronfield.

The company remained in the Marples family until 1962, and following a series of changes of ownership it is now part of Irwin Tools, though still trading with the Marples name.

[1879 p277]

Thomas Turner's company was established in 1802, and their Suffolk Works were built in about 1834 on Suffolk Road, beside the Porter Brook (seen on the left of the works). The 1879 Guide points out that they adjoin the 'new' Midland Railway Station. The railway can be seen in the background, and the goods yard to the left of Porter Brook. The site is now a multi-storey car park

[1879 p265]

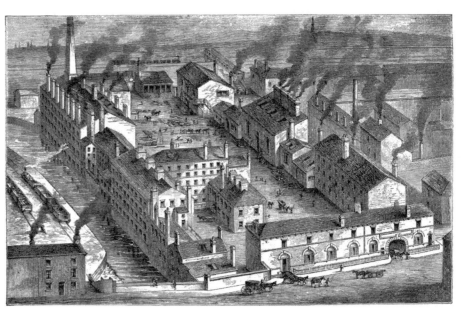

SUFFOLK WORKS—MESSRS. THOMAS TURNER AND CO.

ALBION STEEL WORKS—MESSRS. J. R. SPENCER AND SON

The 1879 Guide shows the Albion Steel Works on Pea Croft (now Solly Street) operated by J. R. Spencer and Sons, a company founded in 1749. St. Vincent's Roman Catholic Church was built next to the works in the 1850s.

The company had a high reputation for the manufacture of files, but also produced cutlery, shovels and steel wire.

The site of the works is now a car park.

[1879 p267]

The forging and grinding shop shown on the right was that of James Howarth & Sons at Broomspring Works, Bath Street. Howarth's were makers of edge tools and joiners' tools, set up by James Howarth in 1835. They also made ice skates.

The company was wound-up in 1911, and the Bath Street Works were taken on by Viners (originally Vieners). The works were acquired by Robert Sorby & Sons in 1922.

The site is now Headford Mews behind the Kings Court DWP Offices on Hanover Way.

[1879 p270, 1889 p173]

FORGING AND GRINDING AT MESSRS. JAMES HOWARTH AND SONS'.

FRONT VIEW OF MESSRS JOSEPH RODGERS AND SONS' WORKS, NORFOLK STREET.

The star and maltese cross mark was first registered by Joseph Rodgers in 1764. Rodgers originally worked in Hawley Croft, and in 1780 the firm moved to No. 6, Norfolk Street. It was this site which expanded to create the works shown in these illustrations.

The property was sold in 1929, and the site is now under Mecca Bingo on Arundel Gate.

In the 20th century there was a general decline in the cutlery industry, and in 1986 Joseph Rodgers & Sons and their competitor George Wostenholm were bought by the Eggington Group.

The group continue to produce knives under the original names of the companies.

[1862 p139] & [1879 p255]

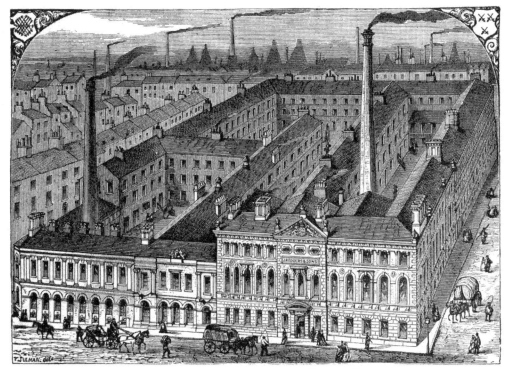

MESSRS. JOSEPH RODGERS AND SONS, NORFOLK-STREET.

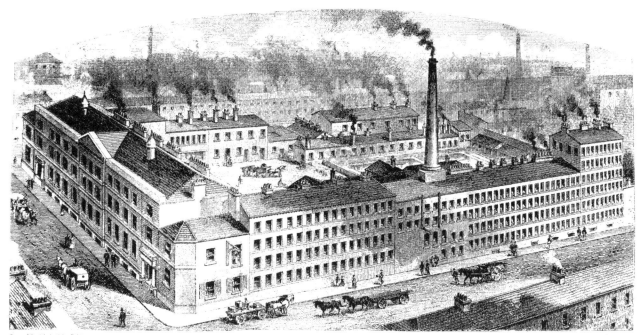

WASHINGTON WORKS.—MESSRS. GEORGE WOSTENHOLM AND SON LIMITED.

George Wolstenholme (b. 1717) started making cutlery in Stannington in 1745 . His grandson, another George (1755-1833), moved to Sheffield and in 1810 built Rockingham Works, in Rockingham Street. It is said that his name was too long to fit on smaller knives, therefore the family name was changed to Wostenholm.

The I*XL mark, first registered in 1787, was assigned to the next George Wostenholm (1800-1876) in 1831. He had completed his apprenticeship with his father in 1826, and moved to set up him own factory at Washington Works in 1848.

Washington Works were a speculative development and were one of the first large cutlery works built close to the centre of Sheffield. They were not an immediate success until taken on by Wostenholm. The works fronted onto Wellington Street, and as the company prospered they were repeatedly expanded to fill the block between Bowden Street and Eldon Street.

The works were demolished in 1976.

The main market for Wostenholm's products was the United States and this is reflected in the name George chose for his works. Wostenholm's home at Kenwood Park in Nether Edge, was also named after a town he had visited in up-state New York during his frequent visits to the country.

[1889 p166, 1899 p260] & [1862 p141]

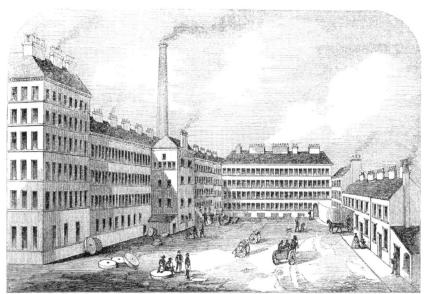

BACK VIEW OF WASHINGTON WORKS.—MESSRS. G. WOSTENHOLM AND SON, CUTLERY MANUFACTURERS.

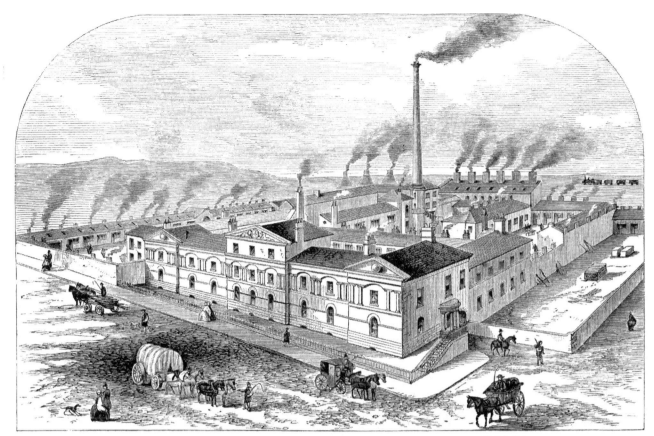

GLOBE WORKS.—MESSRS. J. WALTERS AND CO., CUTLERY MANUFACTURERS AND MERCHANTS.

Globe Works on Penistone Road were built in 1825 for the edge tool makers Ibbotson and Roebank. As with many works at that time, the owner lived on the premises, and the steps and porch on the side of the building, to the right of the façade, gave access to the owner's house.

John Walters and Co. were working in Calver Street in 1847, and moved from the city centre to Globe Works in 1852 to make table and spring knives, steel and tools. They specialised in making Bowie Knives for the American market.

From 1865 the works were in several hands, until in 1970 there was a proposal to demolish them to make way for a new ring road. They survived and were restored in 1987, including a visitor centre and pub. In the 1990s they were refurbished as a business centre and offices. They are now Grade II* listed.

[1862 p143]

TABLE BLADE FORGING—MESSRS. M. HUNTER AND SON.

The Hunter family included five successive Michaels, all involved in some way in the cutlery business.

The company ran the Talbot Works on Sheldon Row, and later on Andrew Street, both off the Wicker, and by 1879 on Saville Street. They were the first works to apply the tilt hammer to table blade forging, and to use steel for the whole blade and tang avoiding unnecessary welding. Such innovation was the basis of their success. They traded world-wide and especially with South America – one of their marks was "LLAMA".

[1879 p258]

Andrew Jackson Jordan was born in Baltimore in 1845. In 1871, as a cutlery retailer in St. Louis he mostly dealt in German goods, but believed that the best quality was made in Sheffield. He therefore moved to Sheffield in 1885 and set up his own works in Radford Street, Netherthorpe, making his 'AaAA1' razors. He soon moved to East India Works on Bakers Hill in the town centre, and by 1900 his works had moved to Furnival Street. Jordan left Sheffield in 1920 and died in 1929. His Sheffield business did not survive his passing.

[1889 p167]

EAST INDIA WORKS.

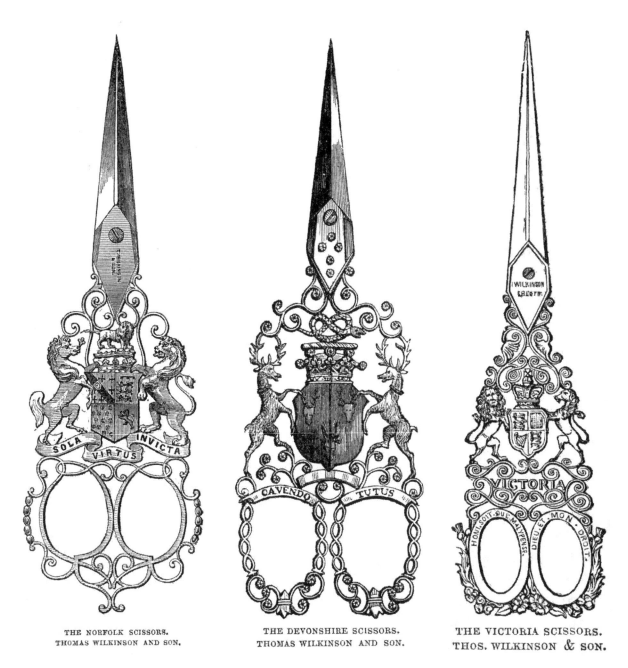

THE NORFOLK SCISSORS.
THOMAS WILKINSON AND SON.

THE DEVONSHIRE SCISSORS.
THOMAS WILKINSON AND SON.

THE VICTORIA SCISSORS.
THOS. WILKINSON & SON.

The firm of Thomas Wilkinson & Son, Manufacturers of Tailors Shears and Scissors, was founded in the 18th century and was appointed Manufacturers of Scissors in Ordinary to Her Majesty Queen Victoria and Cutlers to H.R.H. Prince Albert in 1840.

The 1862 Guide gave the above three examples of presentation scissors made by the firm based in New Church Street to the north of St. Paul's Church (p16), now the site of the Town Hall. The Victoria Scissors were presented to the Queen in 1837 on her coronation. They were designed by George Wilkinson, who became Master Cutler in 1862, and took six weeks to make.

Thomas Wilkinson & Son are now part of William Whiteley & Sons, and are still producing scissors.

[1862 p145] & [1862 p146]

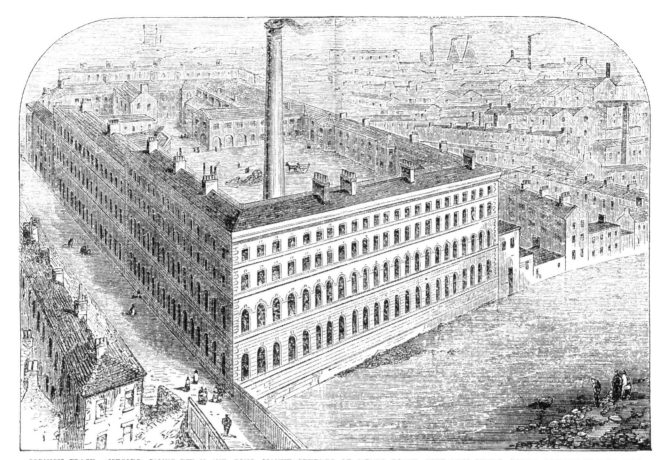

CORNISH PLACE.—MESSRS. JAMES DIXON AND SONS, MANUFACTURERS OF SILVER PLATE, BRITANNIA METAL GOODS, POWDER FLASKS, ETC.

James Dixon and Thomas Smith set up business in Silver Street in 1805 making Britannia metal, pewter-ware and Old Sheffield Plate. In 1822 James Dixon set up his own works in Cornish Place on the Don above Kelham Island. The name 'Cornish' is thought to relate to the 98% of tin used in Britannia metal.

'Old Sheffield Plate' consisted of a layer of silver fused to a block of copper and rolled to form a sheet. It had been invented in Sheffield in 1742 by Thomas Boulsover (1705-88) as a cheaper alternative to solid silver. In the 1840s electro-plating had been developed as a cheaper process, and in the 1850s James Dixon started to use 'nickel silver', an alloy of nickel, copper and zinc, to replace the copper base.

The 1862 illustration above shows Cornish Place, with the River Don and Ball Street bridge in the foreground. The chimney and the main L-shaped block was added in 1851-4 when the works were converted to steam power. The 1879 view (right) shows the works from the south-east with Cornish Street and Green Lane in the foreground.

Production at Cornish Place ended in 1992, and the buildings were converted into apartments.

[1862 p169] & [1879 p287, 1889 p179, 1899 p250]

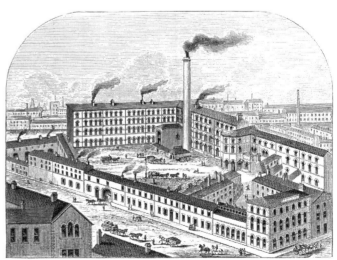

CORNISH WORKS—MESSRS. JAMES DIXON AND SONS.

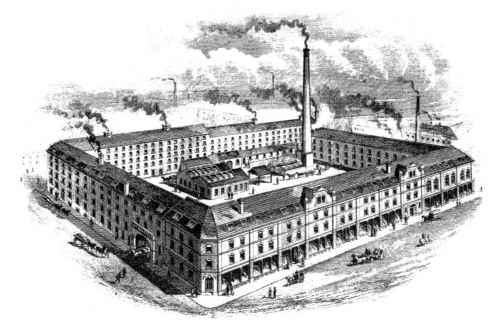

VIEW OF WᴹHUTTON & SONS' WORKS, WEST STꜞ SHEFFIELD.

William Hutton began work as a silversmith in 1800 in Birmingham, and moved to Sheffield in 1832. The company became William Hutton and Sons in 1870 and transferred from the High Street to their West Street works in 1882.

The company failed in 1930 and was absorbed into James Dixon and Sons.

'Hutton's Buildings' still form the north side of West Street, between Orange Street and Rockingham Street.

[1889 p183]

In 1847 John Round set up a workshop attached to his house in Tudor Street, and this became Tudor Works, shown on the right. The works specialised in silver plating and German Silver (nickel silver) principally making spoons and forks.

In 1874 the firm became a limited company and the Round family ceased to have an active role in the business. In 1898 the cutlery and spoon & fork departments moved to Rockingham Street, and in the 1930s the business was purchased by Joseph Rodgers & Sons and transferred to their Pond Hill Works.

[1862 p173]

TUDOR SPOON AND FORK WORKS.—MESSRS. J. ROUND AND SON.

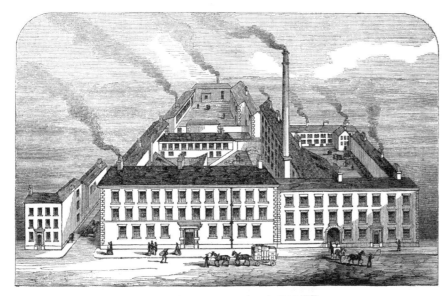

ELECTRO-PLATING WORKS.—MESSRS. WALKER AND HALL.

George Walker set up his plating business in Sheffield in 1845 and was joined in 1853 by Henry Hall. They set up their works in Howard Street in the centre of Sheffield. The firm became a limited company in 1920 and in 1963 became part of British Silverware Ltd. with Mappin & Webb and Elkington & Co.

Their specialities were electro-plating in gold and silver, though they were also known for electro-bronzing using a mixture of zinc and copper.

By the end of the 19th century the Walker and Hall works still stood on the junction of Howard Street and Eyre Street and were dominated by a nine storey central block. They were demolished in 1965, and are now the site of the Winter Gardens.

[1862 p171]

The Atlas Brass Works were on Saville Street opposite the Cyclops Works. Though trading under the name of Benjamin Vickers, they were owned by John Brown (1815-82), the mayor of Chesterfield in 1879-82.

The premises were let in 1869 and sold in 1878.

[1862 p178]

ATLAS BRASS WORKS.—MESSRS. B. VICKERS AND CO.

Henry Elliot Hoole's Green Lane Works were re-built in 1860 with an elegant arched entrance to celebrate Hoole's term as mayor of Sheffield in that year. The firm was started in 1795 and made stove-grates, fenders and fire-irons.

The frontage includes statues of Hephæstus, the Greek god of fire and patron of metal workers, and of Athene, the goddess of heroic endeavour, thought to be by Alfred Stevens, an eminent sculptor who had designed for Hoole in the 1850s.

The works continued to make stove grates and fenders until 1930, and until 1948 the Ibbotson Brothers group produced files on the site. In 1948 the works were purchased by W.A. Tyzack who made agricultural tools until production ended in 2007.

[1862 p174]

ENTRANCE TO GREEN-LANE WORKS.—MESSRS. H. E. HOOLE AND CO.

The entrance, now Grade II* listed, and a workshop block, seen in the left in the interior view, still exist, though the gatehouse is on the 'buildings at risk' register.

In 2012 a planning application was approved to build 107 houses on this site and the adjacent Eagle Works. The development will retain the historic buildings, converting the gateway into a shop and restaurant.

[1862 p175]

GREEN-LANE WORKS.—MESSRS. H. E. HOOLE AND CO., STOVE GRATE MANUFACTURERS.

STOVE.—MESSRS. ROBERTSON AND CARR.

In 1850, the stove grate and fender makers Alexander Robertson, Henry Smith Carr and Henry Francis Steel, moved from their Union Street Works and Rockingham Foundry to new and bigger premises at Chantrey Works in Sylvester Street, close to St. Mary's Church, Bramall Lane. The works stood on the banks of the Porter Brook, which in those days was not culverted as it is now.

Steel left the partnership in 1858 and the illustration from the 1862 Guide shows a grate made by Robertson and Carr.

The firm specialised in 'goods of high artistic merit … striking effects being produced by the contrast of burnished steel with jet black surfaces, and with bronze, ormolu, and other rich metals'. The grate shown above is similar to one exhibited in the 1862 International Exhibition and described as "A Pillar Grate in the Tudor style, adapted for a baronial mansion. The body, bars and dogs are cast-iron. The balls and jewelled ornamentation are malleable iron, being susceptible of a high polish, contrasting with the deep black of the body of the grate."

[1862 p177]

The partnership of Robertson and Carr was dissolved in 1874 and by 1879 the firm was run by Carr's sons, Henry Herbert and Charles Clement, and William Thomas Webster. By 1885 Webster and Charles Clement Carr (trading as Carr and Webster) had to pay off their creditors, and in 1896 William Summers (trading as Clement Carr and Company, still at Chantrey Works) applied to be discharged as a bankrupt.

The site of the works became the Crown Steel Works and is now occupied by the City Walk apartments.

[1879 p283]

BRONZE STOVE—MESSRS. CARR BROS. AND WEBSTER.

SHOW ROOMS—MESSRS. STEEL AND GARLAND.

Steel and Garland were established in 1855, and Wharncliffe Works, on Green Lane, were built in 1861. Like many other manufacturers in Sheffield, the firm had their own showrooms attached to the works.

The company was wound-up in 1905, and re-formed several times through the 20th century.

The buildings still stand, and are Grade II listed, but are no longer in use.

[1879 p284]

An unusual aspect of Sheffield's steel industry was the making of crinolines. In the 1862 Guide Robert and George Gray (in partnership with John Henderson) were said to be the main manufacturer, with works at Pond Hill and Castle Mills. The Guide describes the cutting, hardening and tempering of the steel strip, and inserting the cotton bound strip into skirts made of materials such as calico, net, alpaca and mohair.

The partnership of R. and G. Gray was dissolved in 1863, though Robert Gray continued the manufacturing business, and the partners continued to run a drapers shop in the Victoria Buildings in West Street.

[1862 p160]

CRINOLINE ROOM.—MESSRS R. AND G. GRAY AND CO.

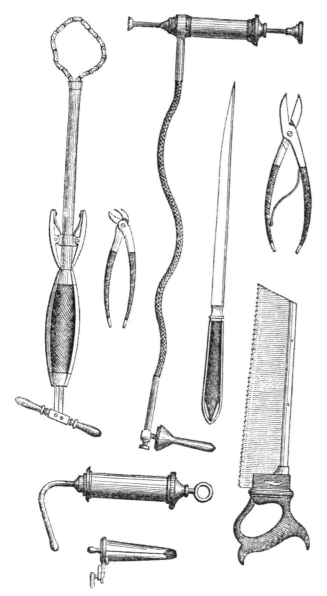

SURGICAL INSTRUMENTS. MR. W. SKIDMORE.

In the 1862 Guide, surgical instruments warranted a separate heading since in that year Sheffield manufacturers had for the first time sent their products under their own name to the International Exhibition. Previously, instruments made in Sheffield had been sold and exhibited as the products of their London merchants.

William Skidmore was active from the 1840s until his death in 1880 as a maker of surgical, dental and veterinary instruments. In the 1850s he had worked from Fitzwilliam Street, and by 1862 he was working from 'Enema Works' in Cemetery Road and from Pearl Street in Sharrow.

The Guide goes on to describe the use of some of the instruments, though it suggests that several are 'self-explanatory'.

The name of William Skidmore & Co. Ltd. still exists as part of B. Braun Medical Ltd. based in Chapletown.

[1862 p166]

EYE DOUCHE.—MR. W. SKIDMORE.

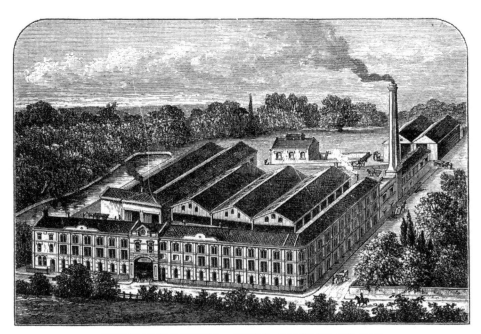

MEERSBROOK TANNERY.—MESSRS. F. COLLEY AND SON.

Sheffield's industry required many supporting enterprises. One such was the manufacture of leather belts to operate machinery, and one producer was Francis Colley of Meersbrook Tannery. The tannery was built in 1870 and stood on the corner of Chesterfield Road and Valley Road in Heeley.

In the early 20th century the area was converted to housing as Arthington, Southall and Whiting Streets, though the frontage was retained and is now known as Meersbrook Buildings.

[1879 p295]

In 1848, the partnership was dissolved between Edward Allatt and John Manuel, Cabinet Makers and Upholsterers of Devonshire Street. John Manuel carried on the business, and by 1871 he and his son, also John, were running the Devonshire Cabinet Works at the junction of Division Street and Carver Street.

The site is now occupied by offices and is known as Star House.

[1879 p299]

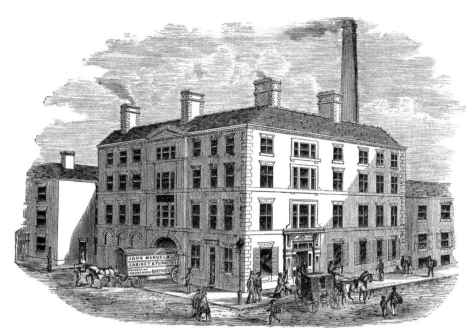

DEVONSHIRE CABINET WORKS—MESSRS. JOHN MANUEL AND SON.

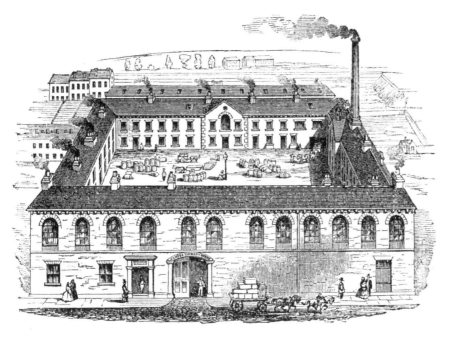

George Bassett started his confectionary business in 1842, and in 1852 built the works shown here on Portland Street, close to the General Infirmary. Bassett's famous product, Liquorice Allsorts was created here in 1899, when a box of samples was dropped and mixed.

A new factory was built in Owlerton in 1900, and the firm moved there fully in 1934. The Portland Street site is now housing on Philadelphia Gardens.

In 1989 Bassett's were acquired by Cadbury-Schweppes , later part of Kraft Foods, and are now part of Mondelēz International.

CONFECTIONERY WORKS.—MESSRS. GEORGE BASSETT AND CO.

COMFIT ROOM.—MESSRS. GEORGE BASSETT AND CO.

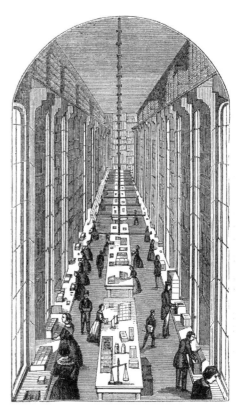

CONFECTIONERY WAREHOUSE.—MESSRS. G. BASSETT AND CO.

[1862 p180], [1862 p181, 1879 p297], and [1862 p182, 1879 p298]

Parks and the Suburbs

CONSERVATORIES—BOTANICAL GARDENS.

THE MANOR LODGE.

The Manor Lodge is one of the few reminders of an important piece of Sheffield's history – the imprisonment of Mary Queen of Scots at Sheffield Manor between 1569 and 1584. At the time, the Manor was a fairly new building dating from 1516, and the 'Turret House' was added in 1574.

The manor was largely demolished in 1706 and the remaining buildings fell into decay. The 1879 Guide describes the work done in 1873 to restore the 'Lodge', as the Turret House was then called.

The interior view of the Lodge shows the elaborate plaster ceiling of the second floor room.

The arms on the right wall are those of the Talbot family, and are in fact the upper part of a fireplace restored in 1873 - this image must therefore predate that work .

[1879 p38, 1889 p18, 1899 p24] & [1879 p39, 1889 p19, 1899 p25]

ROOM IN MANOR LODGE.

THE MONTGOMERY MONUMENT.

James Montgomery (1771-1854), though not a native of Sheffield, achieved his fame as a poet, editor, publisher and philanthropist while living in the town. For much of this time he lived and worked on Hartshead (p40), moving in 1835 to No. 4, The Mount in Broomhill.

He died in 1854, and this bronze statue on a granite plinth was erected in the General Cemetery, near to the Cemetery Road entrance, in 1861. The statue was cast by the Coalbrook Dale Iron Company.

The monument was moved to the east side of Sheffield Cathedral in 1971.

[1862 p69, 1879 p123]

Between July and October 1832, 402 people died in Sheffield during a major outbreak of cholera. Many were buried in an isolated area of Clay Wood opposite the Shrewsbury Hospital on Norfolk Road.

The epidemic led to the creation of local Boards of Health to manage the response to such emergencies.

In 1834 work began to build a memorial to those who died, and to lay out the area as a memorial garden. The gardens were given to the city by the Duke of Norfolk in 1930.

The monument was struck by lightning in 1990 and rebuilding was completed in 2006.

[1862 p72, 1879 p125]

THE CHOLERA MONUMENT.

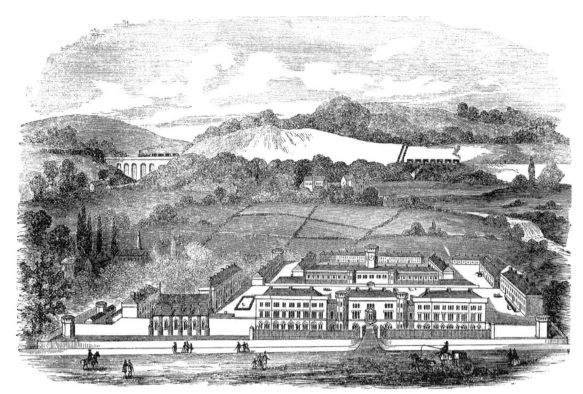

BIRD'S EYE VIEW OF THE SHEFFIELD BARRACKS AND NEIGHBOURING SCENERY.

The 'new barracks' at Hillsborough were completed in 1850 to replace the 'old barracks' which stood further along Langsett Road. The old site is marked only by the name of Barrack Lane. Features of the new barracks can still be recognized in the supermarket and offices which now occupy the site.

Beyond the barracks, the open fields stretching to the river now include the Owlerton Stadium and Hillsborough College. The railway in the distance was then the Manchester, Sheffield & Lincolnshire Railway running over the Wardsend Arches (Herries Road viaduct) and on to Woodhead and Manchester.

[1862 p68]

As well as the army units stationed at the Hillsborough Barracks from 1858 through to 1930, Sheffield also raised a number of volunteer units including the Fourth West Yorkshire Royal Artillery Volunteers established in 1859. Their headquarters in Edmund Road opened in 1880 and included the hall shown, which could seat 2,500 people .

The building is still standing. The hall is now Grade II listed and is used as a garage and workshops.

VOLUNTEER ARTILLERY DRILL HALL

[1889 p58, 1899 p79]

In 1873 the Town Council purchased Weston Hall, the former home of the late Miss Harrison, and its grounds for use as a Public Park and Museum. The park, the first municipal park in the town, was opened to the public in 1875.

A monument was built within the park in 1875 in memory of Godfrey Sykes, a local artist and second master of the School of Art (p29) who had died in 1866 while superintending the decoration of the South Kensington Museum (now the V&A).

The column is made in white terracotta and includes a medallion portrait of the artist.

The monument was moved in 1982 from close to the Mappin Art Gallery (p110) to a new location 60 m. (65 yds.) to the east, within the park.

A second memorial was also added to the park in 1875 when the monument to Ebenezer Elliott was transferred from the Market Place (p42).

[1879 p129, 1889 p72, 1899 p94]

THE GODFREY SYKES MONUMENT.

The terracotta gateposts of the south-east entrance to the park (by Firth Court) include designs by Godfrey Sykes from his work in South Kensington.

The wrought iron gates were stolen in 1994. They were recovered in 2011, but only after they had already been replaced.

[1879 p128, 1889 p71, 1899 p93]

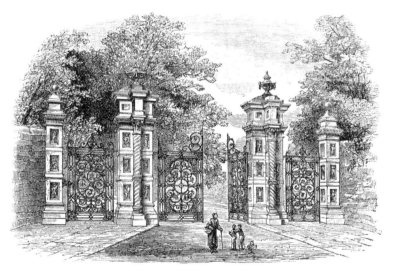

ENTRANCE GATES, WESTON PARK.

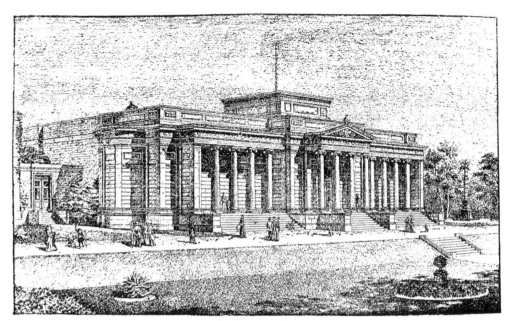

THE MAPPIN ART GALLERY.

The Mappin Art Gallery was built in 1887 alongside the former Weston Hall, by then the City Museum. It housed the art collection bequeathed by John Newton Mappin of the cutlery firm Mappin & Webb.

The illustration shows the Sykes' Monument in its original position to the right of the gallery.

A 1905 proposal to build matching wings to each side of the gallery was not adopted, and in the 1930s the old museum was replaced by the current museum building. A direct hit in the Blitz of 1940 led in major changes to the galleries in the 1950s and '60s. By 2003 the buildings were in a poor state but have now been refurbished and converted to a single entity reopened in 2006 and now known as Weston Park Museum.

[1889 p74]

Meersbrook Hall was built in 1760 for Benjamin Roebuck, a Sheffield merchant and banker.

In 1886 Sheffield Council bought both the house and the land as a public park and to prevent its use for housing.

From 1890 to 1953 the house was the home of the Ruskin Collection now on display in Sheffield's Millennium Gallery. Since 1960 it has housed the City Parks Department.

MEERSBROOK HALL.

[1889 p79]

CONSERVATORIES—BOTANICAL GARDENS.

The Botanical Gardens opened in 1836 in a rural area with uninterrupted views across the Porter valley to the newly laid out General Cemetery.

The gardens were created by the Sheffield Botanical and Horticultural Society and designed by Robert Marnock, whose gardens also include Weston Park. Other than four times a year when the public were admitted, the gardens were only accessible to shareholders and annual subscribers.

In 1844 the gardens were sold to a new company of shareholders at half the original cost, the conservatories were extended, and the present Curator's House was added. Access was still restricted until 1898, when the Town Trust took on the failing enterprise, and free admission was introduced.

The City Council took on the management of the gardens in 1951, and in 1996 a major restoration project began. This was completed in 2005.

[1879 p132, 1889 p76]

Firth Park was originally part of the estate of Page Hall, the home of the founder of the silver-plate manufacturers James Dixon and Sons. On the death of Dixon's son, the estate was purchased by Mark Firth, and 36 acres (14.5 ha.) were donated to the town as a public park. The park were opened in 1875 by the Prince of Wales.

The building shown, now known as the Clock Tower, still stands on Firth Park Road and is used by Community groups

[1879 p133, 1889 p77, 1899 p100]

ENTRANCE TO FIRTH PARK.

ENDCLIFFE WOOD AND DAM.—DRAWN BY MR. W. NICHOLSON.

These views of Endcliffe Woods in the 1862 Guide were described as having been drawn 'on the wood' (i.e. directly onto the wood engraving block) by a local artist, Walter Nicholson (1835-1901).

The valley, with its grinding wheels and their mill dams, was already a place of recreation as well as a workplace.

[1862 p192, 1879 p301]

Within Endcliffe, there were three dams, the highest, Nether Spur-gear or Greystones Wheel was at one time used for knife grinding. Holme Wheel, whose pond was later used for boating, was also used for grinding knives, and the lowest, Endcliffe Wheel was still in use in 1880 for file grinding. It was later reserved for swimming, but was closed and in-filled in 1938.

[1862 p192, 1879 p302]

VIEW IN ENDCLIFFE WOOD.—DRAWN BY MR. W. NICHOLSGN.

ENDCLIFFE WOOD—NEW ROAD.

In 1885, the woods were purchased by the Corporation of Sheffield, and Endcliffe Park was opened in 1887 to commemorate the Jubilee of Queen Victoria. A secondary reason for the purchase was to enable a new sewer to be built for new housing to the north of the park.

A new 'carriage' road, shown on the left, was also laid out to the south of the park. It was given the name Rustlings Road after Rustlings Farm which stood at its junction with Ecclesall Road.

[1889 p79]

The second view from the 1889 Guide, shown below, shows the upper dam, formerly that of the Nether Spurgear Wheel, which was adapted for waterfowl by adding two artificial islands.

Further land was either purchased or donated over the next 50 years to form a series of contiguous open spaces along the Porter Valley.

Bingham Park was presented by Sir John E. Bingham in 1911, supposedly after he offered to buy his wife a diamond necklace or, if she chose, to buy the land 'for the children of Sheffield'. It was extended to include Shepherd's Wheel in 1927.

Whitely Woods were added in stages in 1898, 1913 and 1932. Finally, in 1938, Forge Dam and the rest of Porter Clough were acquired by the J. G. Graves Charitable Trust.

[1889 p80]

VIEW IN ENDCLIFFE WOOD.

As Sheffield grew through the 19th century, remnants of old parks and farms were gradually destroyed. The Mongomery Oaks (or Brincliffe Oaks) were a remnant which survived in Nether Edge. The trees stood south-west of the junction of Oakdale and Oakhill Roads opposite the former Brincliffe Oaks Hotel, and survived into the 20th century.

The land was part of an estate of building plots laid out in 1853 by the Reform Freehold Building Society (from 1861 the Montgomery Land Society) with the houses being built on the plots by individuals over the succeeding years. The last plots were sold in 1883 and the society was wound-up.

[1879 p192]

MONTGOMERY OAKS.

The stone-built wing added to Carbrook Hall in the 1620s also survived while the town expanded around it. It still stands on Attercliffe Common surrounded by offices and industrial units. It is reputed to be Sheffield's most haunted pub.

The upper room shown in the illustration survives and includes examples of 17th century panelling and plasterwork, thought to be by the same craftsmen who worked on Bolsover Castle.

[1879 p190, 1889 p116, 1899 p156]

UPPER ROOM IN CARBROOK HALL.

THE BIRTHPLACE OF CHANTREY.

Francis Leggatt Chantrey was born in 1781 in a farm house off Cinderhill Lane in the village of Norton, then within Derbyshire.

From these humble beginnings, and starting his working life in a grocer's shop, he rose to be one of the leading sculptors in Britain.

He was knighted in 1835 and died in 1841. He was buried in Norton Churchyard and a memorial obelisk stands close by (p19).

[1879 p197, 1889 p121, 1899 p162]

Beauchief Abbey was founded in 1183 and dedicated to Thomas à Becket who had been murdered in 1170.

The alabaster altar-piece was given to the abbey by Sir Godfrey Foljambe in about 1350. The arms are those of Sir Godfrey (six escallops and the 'jamb' (leg) seen on the right) and of his wife Avice (or Aveline) Ireland (six fleur-de-lis). The same arms can be seen on their mural monument in the south aisle of Bakewell Church.

At some time after the dissolution of the abbey in 1536 the carving was removed to the Foljambe family home at Aldwark and later at Osberton, near Worksop.

[1879 p326]

ALTAR-PIECE FROM BEAUCHIEF ABBEY, NOW AT OSBERTON.

The Surrounding District

WENTWORTH HOUSE.

SHIRECLIFFE.— FROM A SKETCH BY MR. C. THOMPSON.

Shirecliffe is the location of the 'preaching tree' in Ebenezer Elliott's poem 'The Ranter'.

The site shown, by a quarry above Old Park Wood, gave views across Walkley, Stannington and Loxley in the distance, and Hillsborough and Neepsend in the Don valley below. A train on the Manchester, Sheffield & Lincolnshire Railway can just be seen passing the chapel at Wardsend Cemetery.

[1862 p189, 1879 p322, 1889 p195]

Darfield, near Barnsley, is well outside even the modern boundary of Sheffield. It was included in the Guides as the burial place of Ebenezer Elliott, the 'Corn Law Rhymer', who died there in 1849. Elliott was born in Masborough in 1781 and spent most of his life working in the steel trade in Sheffield, living for many years in Upperthorpe. After his death a memorial was erected in the Market Place (p42) and later moved to Weston Park (p109).

[1879 p195, 1889 p119, 1899 p160]

DARFIELD CHURCH.

THE PORTER FALLS.—DRAWN BY MR. W. NICHOLSON.

STANEDGE.—FROM A SKETCH BY MR. W. IBBITT.

Above Endcliffe Woods (p112), the footpath follows the Porter Clough through Whiteley Woods and on to Ringinglow along what is now part of the Sheffield Round Walk.

The valley becomes steeper beyond Forge Mill and in its upper part includes the Porter Falls.

[1862 p193, 1879 p304]

The three Redmires Reservoirs were built in response to the 1832 cholera epidemic to provide clean water to the Hadfield Service Reservoir in Crookes.

The 'causeway' from Stanage towards Sheffield seen in the foreground is part of a medieval pack-horse route over the escarpment from Hathersage.

A milestone added to mark the route in the 1730s now stands in the middle of the upper reservoir.

[1862 p194, 1879 p310]

This view from a sketch by William Ibbitt (1804-1869) shows the escarpment of Stanedge (now generally called Stanage) looking towards High Neb, the highest point in Sheffield.

In the 19th century, the gritstone 'edge' was known for its wild and picturesque views. Nowadays the edge is well known for rock climbing and hang gliding.

[1862 p194, 1879 p311]

REDMIRES RESERVOIRS.—FROM A SKETCH BY MR. W. IBBITT.

VIEW ON THE RIVELIN.

The Rivelin, like the Porter, was both a place of industry and of recreation. The Guides include an eloquent description of the valley by Christopher Thomson (1799-1871), the artist who also produced the illustrations.

An oil painting of this same scene, also by Thomson, is in the Museums Sheffield collection.

[1862 p184, 1879 p306, 1889 p188]

VIEW ON THE RIBBLEDIN.—FROM A SKETCH BY MR. C. THOMSON.

The 'Ribbledin' was not to be found on any maps of the area at the time of the Guides, and though the author states that 'the name is generally accepted by the townfolk' it still remains unmarked.

The stream which joins the Rivelin after it has passed under Manchester Road is more generally called Black Brook, but was named Ribbledin by Ebenezer Elliott in this poem 'The Christening'. The name is said to reflect the sound of the stream.

[1862 p185, 1879 p307, 1889 p189]

WYMING-BROOK.—FROM A SKETCH BY MR. C THOMSON.

In the 1840s two reservoirs were created on the Rivelin to provide water for Sheffield and as 'compensation reservoirs' to regulate the flow of water for the grinding wheels along the valley.

The Wyming Brook is a tributary of the Rivelin which flows into the lower Rivelin Reservoir.

[1862 p187, 1879 p309]

The valley of Wyming Brook was described in the Guides as a 'wild gorge' which 'the tourist may climb by the aid of fallen branches, twigs of trees, and the long grasses and brackens'. The Guides also say that 'Ladies occasionally make the ascent without much difficulty in dry weather'.

There is now a track which follows the valley and can be accessed from car parks off Redmires Road and by the lower Rivelin Dam. The track was built in the early years of the 20th century for use by walkers and by cars, but it is now classed as a bridle way.

The upper part of the valley is a Nature Reserve managed by the Wildlife Trust.

[1879 p308]

WYMING BROOK.

In 1862 the woods at Wharncliffe were open to the public on Mondays and Wednesdays. They were a popular excursion on the Manchester, Sheffield & Lincolnshire Railway from Sheffield to Deepcar Station.

Part of the attraction would have been the legend of 'The Dragon of Wantley', a story told in a poem published in 1765. The dragon lived on the crags and terrorized the neighbourhood devouring children, cattle, forests, and even houses. The dragon was finally defeated by More of More Hall wearing armour made from Sheffield steel.

[1862 p198, 1879 p316, 1889 p194]

WHARNCLIFFE CRAGS AND DRAGON'S DEN.—FROM A SKETCH BY MR. W. IBBITT.

The Table Rock stands above the Dragon's Den on the edge of the crags, overlooking the valleys of the Don and the Little Don to the west. From this same viewpoint looking east it is said that, on a clear day, you can see York Minster and Lincoln Cathedral.

Much of the heath above the crags and the woodland below is now accessible. It is owned by the Forestry Commission and managed as a Local Nature Reserve in partnership with the Wharncliffe Heathlands Trust.

[1862 p197, 1879 p315, 1889 p193]

WHARNCLIFFE, FROM THE TABLE ROCK.—FROM A SKETCH BY MR. W. IBBITT.

Pray for the soyle of
Thomas Woyttelay knyght
for the Kyngys bode to Edward
the forth Richard Therd Hare vii. and Hare viii.
Hows faults God perdon-Whyche
Thomas caused a loge to be made
Hon this crag in mydst of
Wancliff for his plesor to her the
hartes bel in the yere of our
Lord a Thousand ccccc

Wharncliffe Lodge, which stands on the Heath above Wharncliffe Crags, was built by Sir Thomas Wortley in the reign of Henry VIII.

An inscribed slab tells of its origin. Originally exposed to the elements, by 1862 the stone slab was covered by an extension to the lodge, and was protected by a wooden panel.

The text from the slab, transcribed as shown above in the 1899 Guide [1899 p267], reads …

"Pray for the soul of Thomas Wortley Knight of the King's commands to Edward IV, Richard III, Henry VII and Henry VIII whose faults God pardon. Thomas caused a lodge to be made on this crag in the middle of Wharncliffe for his pleasure to hear the hart's call in the year of our Lord 1510."

BOOTS IN WHARNCLIFFE LODGE.

The 1879 Guide tells us that the Lodge was then occupied by a servant of its owner, the Earl of Wharncliffe, and that tea and accommodation could be provided for picnic parties.

As well as the scenery and the history of the lodge, visitors could also view the boots worn by Sir Francis Wortley, the 1st Baronet and a follower of King Charles who fought at Marston Moor and Naseby. Sir Francis was imprisoned in the Tower of London (1644-49) and died in 1652 before the restoration of the monarchy.

[1879 p319]

A further curiosity for the visitors to Wharncliffe was the 'twin tree', a large decaying Oak to which a Birch tree had apparently been grafted. It would appear that the Birch tree was in fact growing from below ground level through the hollow trunk of the Oak.

[1879 p320]

TWIN TREE NEAR WHARNCLIFFE LODGE.

ROTHERHAM INDEPENDENT COLLEGE.

Until 1828 non-conformists were excluded from admission to universities, therefore, in 1795, Rotherham Independent Academy was created in Masborough by Samuel Walker, owner of the Walker Iron Works. Its purpose was to educate young men for ministry in the Independent Church.

In 1876, the College (by then renamed) moved to a new building on Moorgate, but 12 years later, in 1888, it merged with the Airedale Independent College and moved to Bradford.

The building, shown here, was purchased in 1890 by Rotherham Grammar School. The school was established in 1483 and in 1967 was renamed after its founder Thomas Rotherham, a son of the town who had risen to be Archbishop of York.

[1879 p375]

The site of Conisborough Castle was probably fortified soon after the Norman Conquest, and the current castle was built between 1180 and 1190. Though its old name is 'Cyningesburh', a Saxon word meaning 'the king's fortress', it was never a royal residence.

Its last occupant died in 1446 and the castle fell into disuse. Unlike Sheffield Castle, which was destroyed, Conisborough avoided damage after the English Civil War because it was already in a ruinous state.

The Castle is now in the care of English Heritage. The keep has recently been restored and its floors and roof replaced.

[1879 p384, 1889 p225 , 1899 p300]

CONISBROUGH CASTLE.

ROCHE ABBEY.

Roche Abbey, founded in 1147 for the Cistercian monks of St. Mary of the Rock (Roche), sits astride Maltby Dike one mile south of Maltby, hidden among the cliffs of Magnesian Limestone used in its construction.

The Abbey was dissolved in 1538 and the buildings left in ruin. In the 18th century the owner of the land, the 4th Earl of Scarbrough, had the area landscaped by Capability Brown to enhance his family seat at Sandbeck Park. Excavations in the 1920s revealed the almost complete ground-plan of an English Cistercian monastery hidden by the landscaping. The site is now managed by English Heritage.

[1879 p386, 1889 p226]

Wentworth House, now once again known by its original name of Wentworth Woodhouse, was built in the 18th century to replace an earlier Jacobean House, fragments of which can still be seen in the west façade.

Rivalry with the branch of the family who had built the nearby Wentworth Castle at Stainborough led to the building of the east façade (illustrated), one of the longest in Europe.

The family grew rich on the extensive coal reserves under their land and in the 1940s & 50s the park was dug up on government orders for opencast mining. This caused damage to the buildings which is still being fought today.

In 1999 the house was bought by a former architect, Clifford Newbold, and is now open for pre-booked guided tours.

[1879 p377, 1889 p223]

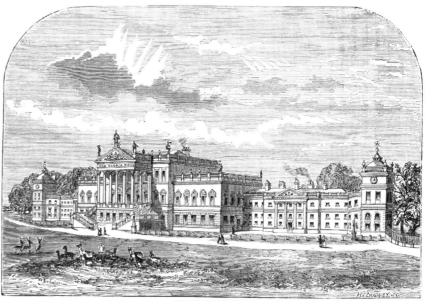

WENTWORTH HOUSE.

WELBECK ABBEY.

The illustration is wrongly captioned in the 1879 Guide as 'Thoresby Hall – From the South-East'.

Welbeck Abbey, the family seat of the Dukes of Portland, is one of the great estates which form The Dukeries in Nottinghamshire. It was built on the site of the original Abbey by Sir Charles Cavendish in the early 1600s.

The estate is renowned for the network of underground rooms and roadways built by the 5th Duke, William John Cavendish-Scott-Bentinck, between 1854 to 1879.

The Abbey is now the home of William Henry Marcello Parente, a descendant on the female line, while the title has passed to another branch, and is now held by Tim Bentinck, an actor better known as David Archer on Radio 4.

[1879 p393, 1889 p229, 1899 p304]

The Major Oak is said to have been named in honour of Major Hayman Rooke (1723-1806) who wrote extensively about the trees of Sherwood Forest.

The Oak stands in the heart of the Forest near to the village of Edwinstowe. Believed to be 1000 years old, since the early 19th century many of the limbs have had to be supported by poles.

[1879 p396]

THE MAJOR OAK.

PRIORY GATEHOUSE, WORKSOP.

The gatehouse to Worksop Priory still stands close to the Priory Church (see on the right of the illustration).

It was built in about 1330 as guest accommodation for visitors to the Priory. The gatehouse survived the dissolution of the priory since it was in use as a school.

The market cross (on the left) was moved here in the 19th century and the shaft was renovated in the 20th.

[1879 p390, 1889 p227, 1899 p302]

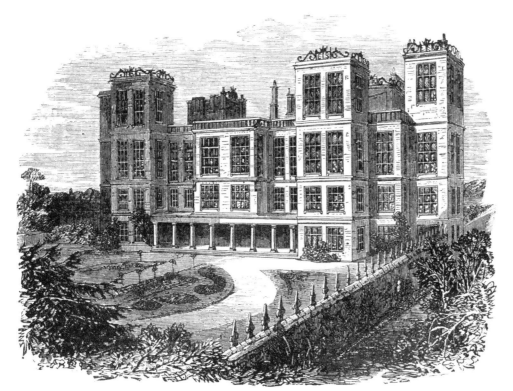

HARDWICK HALL.

After four advantageous marriages, Elizabeth Talbot, 'Bess of Hardwick', Countess of Shrewsbury (~1521-1608), was the richest woman in England other than Queen Elizabeth. In 1590, after the death of her fourth husband, George Talbot, the 6th Earl of Shrewsbury, she set about building a new house next to her old home, the 'old' Hardwick Hall.

The 'new' hall was built for Bess in the 1590s by Robert Smythson, who went on to design Wollaton Hall, near Nottingham, and whose son John rebuilt Bolsover Castle during the early 1600s.

Hardwick Hall is said to have 'more glass than wall' and is a prime example of the new style of architecture brought in from Europe during the reign of Elizabeth I. Houses no longer needed to be fortresses, their purpose was to display the wealth and status of the owner.

Hardwick Hall stands largely unchanged dominating the limestone escarpment south of Bolsover. The 'Old Hall' is now in the care of English Heritage, and since 1959 the 'new' hall and grounds have been managed by the National Trust.

[1879 p354, 1889 p216] &

[1879 p355, 1889 p217, 1899 p291]

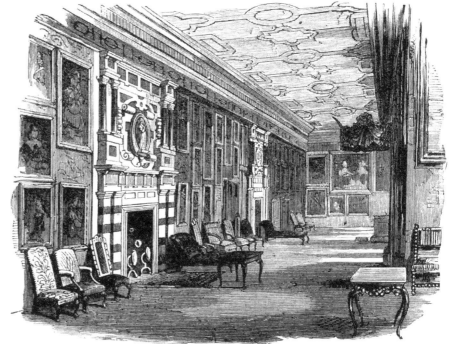

HARDWICK HALL—THE DRAWING ROOM.

CHATSWORTH HOUSE.

Building of the first Chatsworth House by Sir William Cavendish, the second husband of Bess of Hardwick, began in 1553 and was completed by Bess in the 1560s. The house passed to their eldest son, Henry, and was then bought by the second son, another William, who became the 1st Earl of Devonshire in 1618.

Bess's house was replaced by the main part of the current house begun in 1687 by the 4th Earl. In 1694 he was made the 1st Duke of Devonshire under William of Orange as a reward for his role in the 'Glorious Revolution' of 1688.

The Hunting Tower, seen in the distance in the illustration, and Queen Mary's Bower (not shown) are remnants from the Bess's time.

[1879 p331, 1889 p203]

The State Bedroom was originally constructed for a visiting monarch by the 1st Duke, and included a bed which cost £470 and was the most expensive piece of furniture in the house. It was probably never used. The bed's canopy is now at Hardwick Hall and the bed was replaced in 1760 by the bed in which George II died. The bed was a gift to the 4th Duke after the King's death. In 1913 the State Bedroom was finally used by a reigning monarch during the visit of King George V and Queen Mary.

The illustration given here shows the room as it was in the mid 19th century, without the bed, which was in the adjoining Scarlet Room. The chairs either side of the canopy are the coronation 'thrones' of King George III and Queen Charlotte.

[1879 p334, 1899 p276]

CHATSWORTH—THE OLD STATE BEDROOM.

THE BRIDGE AT CHATSWORTH.

In 1758, the 4th Duke commissioned Lancelot 'Capability' Brown to transform the setting of the house into the park landscape seen today.

Roads were closed, trees were planted, the river was modified, and new bridges were built. The bridge shown here on the main approach to the house was designed to provide visitors with a picturesque view of the west front of the house.

This bridge and the 'One Arch' bridge at the southern end of the park, were designed by James Paine (1717–89) who was also responsible for the Stables and other buildings in the park, and for modifications to the house.

[1879 p338, 1889 p207, 1899 p279]

HOUSE IN CHATSWORTH PARK.

Barbrook House, the Italianate house shown in this illustration, was built in 1842 for Joseph Paxton (1803-1865), then the head gardener at Chatsworth. It was designed by Paxton and his architectural assistant John Robertson, and stood near to the kitchen gardens between Chatsworth House and Baslow.

The house was demolished in about 1950 and the old kitchen gardens are now a caravan site. The distinctive 'White Lodge' built in 1855 still stands at the entrance to the kitchen garden from the park.

[1879 p332]

EDENSOR CHURCH AND VILLAGE.

Towards the end of the 18th century the freehold of parts of Edensor village became part of the Chatsworth estate. During Capability Brown's remodelling of the park, the old village was left virtually untouched - only a few buildings at the eastern end of the village were demolished to improve the view from the house.

The main changes to Edensor began in 1817 and continuing through the 1830s. The buildings seen today were built between 1839 and 1841 using designs by John Robertson. Not all were newly built, some, such as the Post Office (now the Tea Rooms), were modifications of original houses.

The church was not changed until the 1860s when much of it was demolished and replaced using a design by Sir George Gilbert Scott.

[1879 p337, 1889 p206, 1899 p280]

The 1879 and 1899 Guides give picturesque descriptions of Monsal Dale without mentioning the railway viaduct which many would now regard as one of its highlights.

The viaduct was built in 1862 as part of the rail link from Bakewell to Buxton.

The line closed in 1968, and the viaduct is now part of the Monsal Trail.

[1879 p362, 1889 p220, 1899 p295]

MONSAL DALE.

HADDON HALL.

Haddon Hall was the home of the Vernon family from the 13th century, and came to the Manners family by the (supposed) elopement and marriage of Dorothy Vernon and John Manners in 1563.

The hall is essentially a mediaeval manor house which evolved until the 1640s when a later John Manners, then the Earl of Rutland, later the 1st Duke, moved with his family to Belvoir Castle.

[1879 p342, 1889 p209]

The hall remained intact and largely untouched until the 1920s when the 9th Duke made it his life's work to restore the buildings as faithfully as possible.

The gateway shown on the right is the original entrance to the Hall under the Eagle Tower at the northern corner of the upper courtyard. Public access is now via the north-west tower and the lower courtyard.

[1879 p339]

THE GATEWAY—HADDON.

THE CHAPEL—HADDON HALL.

In the 19th century, the walls of the chapel (shown on the left) would have shown only traces of the 15th century wall paintings revealed by the 9th Duke's restoration.

The hall is now the home of Lord Edward Manners, brother of the 11th Duke of Rutland. It is open to the public during the summer months and in December.

[1879 p340]

Bibliography

A wide variety of sources were used in writing this book, many were internet based, including Wikipedia. Wherever possible details have been checked with other, possibly more reliable, sources, including those listed below. The list is by no means exhaustive, but may serve as a starting point for interested readers.

Web-sites

BBC 'Your Paintings' – a partnership with the Public Catalogue Foundation - www.bbc.co.uk/arts/yourpaintings/

Grace's Guide – a useful collection of information on industrial history - www.gracesguide.co.uk

London Gazette – a searchable archive covering 1665 to the present day, especially useful in the 19th century for information on partnerships and insolvency - www.thegazette.co.uk

National Library of Scotland, Maps – easy browsing access to historic '6 inch' and mid 20th century '2.5 inch' OS maps of England and Wales (as well as many maps of Scotland) - maps.nls.uk/series/

Old-Maps – really a sales site, but allows browse access to large scale OS maps from 1853 to the late 20th century – www.old-maps.co.uk

Picture Sheffield - run by Sheffield Local Studies Library, providing a wide range of photographs, often annotated, and also high resolution browsing of many old maps of Sheffield (1736-1883) - www.picturesheffield.com

Books

[IA] indicates that the book is currently available online on the 'Internet Archive' (archive.org).
[BL] indicates that the book is currently available as a download from the British Library (www.bl.uk), and as a paper reprint.

'Chatsworth, a Landscape History', by John Barnatt and Tom Williamson, 2005, Windgather Press, Macclesfield.

'Historical memorials of Beauchief Abbey', by Sidney Oldall Addy, 1878, James Parker and Co., Oxford. [IA]

'Illustrated Guide to Chatsworth' by Llewellynn Jewitt, 1872, J C Bates, Buxton. [IA]

'Illustrated Guide to Haddon' by Llewellynn Jewitt, 1871, Virtue and Co., London. [IA]

'Illustrated Guide to Sheffield and Neighbourhood', 1862, Pawson and Brailsford, Sheffield. [BL]

'Illustrated Guide to Sheffield and The Surrounding District', edited by John Taylor, 1879, Pawson and Brailsford, Sheffield. [IA] [BL]

'Illustrated Guide to Sheffield and Neighbourhood', 1889, Pawson and Brailsford, Sheffield

'Illustrated Guide to Sheffield and Neighbourhood', 1899, Pawson and Brailsford, Sheffield.

'**Official Illustrated Guide to the Great Northern Railway**' by George Measom, 1861, Griffin, Bohn and Co., London. [IA]

'**Oil Paintings in Public Ownership, South Yorkshire: Sheffield**', by The Public Catalogue Foundation, 2012, - see also the BBC 'Your Paintings' web-site (www.bbc.co.uk/arts/yourpaintings/)

'**Sheffield and its Neighbourhood – Photographically Illustrated**' by Theophilus Smith, 1865, A W Bennett, London. [BL]

'**Sheffield artists, 1840-1940**', by Hilary Wills, 1996, Basement Gallery, Sheffield.

'**Sheffield in Tudor and Stuart Times**' by David Bostwick, 1985, Sheffield City Museums.

'**Sheffield, Pevsner Architectural Guide**', by Ruth Harman and John Minnis, 2004, Yale University Press.

'**Sheffield Steel**', by Kenneth C. Barraclough, 1976, Sheffield City Museums.

'**Stately Homes of England**', by Llewellynn Jewitt & Samuel Carter Hall, Series 1, 1874, Virtue and Co., London. [BL download 'lsidyv31610a04-l'] (includes Hardwick Hall, Haddon Hall and Chatsworth).

'**Stately Homes of England**', by Llewellynn Jewitt & Samuel Carter Hall, Series 2, 1877, Virtue and Co., London. [BL download 'lsidyv3095def5-ll'] (includes Welbeck Abbey).

'**The Great Sheffield Picture Show**' by David Bostwick, 1989, Sheffield City Museums.

Index

Made in the USA
Charleston, SC
10 July 2014